2 to 22 DAYS IN FRANCE

THE ITINERARY PLANNER

1992 Edition

RICK STEVES
and
STEVE SMITH

John Muir Publications
Santa Fe, New Mexico

Originally published as *22 Days in France*

Other JMP travel guidebooks by Rick Steves
  Asia Through the Back Door (with John Gottberg)
  Europe Through the Back Door
  Europe 101: History, Art, and Culture for the Traveler
    (with Gene Openshaw)
  Mona Winks: Self-Guided Tours of Europe's Top Museums
    (with Gene Openshaw)
  2 to 22 Days in Europe
  2 to 22 Days in Great Britain
  2 to 22 Days in Germany, Austria, and Switzerland
  2 to 22 Days in Norway, Sweden, and Denmark
  2 to 22 Days in Spain and Portugal

John Muir Publications, P.O. Box 613, Santa Fe, NM 87504

1992 Edition

ISSN 1059-8278
ISBN 1-56261-025-2

Distributed to the book trade by
W.W. Norton & Company, Inc.
New York, New York

Design Mary Shapiro
Maps David C. Hoerlein
Cover photo Rick Steves
Typography Copygraphics, Inc.
Printer Banta Company

Thanks to Steve's wife, Karen Lewis, for her help on covering
the cuisine of France.

*Although the authors and publisher have made every effort to
provide accurate, up-to-date information, they accept no
responsibility for loss, injury, or inconvenience sustained by
any person using this book.*

CONTENTS

22 Days in France Route

CHANNEL
BELG.
ENGLISH
D-DAY
BEACHES — HONFLEUR
LUX.
MONT ST-
MICHEL
• ROUEN
REIMS
VERDUN
Normandy
Champagne
DINAN •
Brittany
VERSAILLES
PARIS
Alsace
(START/FINISH)
STRAS-
BOURG
COLMAR
W.
Loire
GER.
TOURS
AMBOISE
DIJON
Burgundy
BEAUNE
ATLANTIC
SWITZ.
ANNECY •
CHAMONIX
OCEAN
• BRANTÔME
Alps
Dordogne
SARLAT
ITALY
• CAHORS
ALBI
Provence
• AVIGNON
MONACO
CARCASSONNE
ARLES
NICE
Pyrénées
MED.
Côte d'Azur
SPAIN
SEA
DCH

O KM 100 200
O MI 50 100

My compliments. You've made a great choice—France is Europe's most diverse, tastiest, and, in many ways, most exciting country to explore. Europe's largest nation, it has over 210,000 square miles, 58 million people, and 460 different cheeses. You'll find three distinct mountain ranges—the Alps, Pyrénées, and Massif Central—and the remarkably different Atlantic and Mediterranean coastlines, as well as exciting cities and sleepy villages. From its Swiss-like Alps to its Italian-feeling Riviera and from the Spanish Pyrenees to das German Alsace, you can stay in France and feel like you've sampled much of Europe.

This book organizes France into an efficient, enjoyable, and diverse 22-day adventure. This tried and tested step-by-step plan hits the famous must-see sights and the off-beat charms of France—from the cliff-hanging castles of the Pyrénées to the scalps of the Alps, along both coastlines, and through France's most characteristic cities and villages. You'll sample much of France, from the art treasures of magnificent Paris to the unforgettable cuisine and wine of villages that somehow missed the modern parade. Join us.

This book is the tour guide in your pocket. It lets you be the chef by giving you the 22 most exciting days in France, with suggested daily menus to get the most out of each day and lots of "franc" advice on cheap travel.

The 2 to 22 Days series is for do-it-yourselfers who want the organization and smoothness of a tour, without the straitjacket. It's like having your quiche and eating it, too.

This plan offers maximum thrills per kilometer, minute, and franc. It's designed for travel by rental car or train. You can even do both—car and train—as the French rail system now offers an inexpensive and very flexible rail/drive package. The pace is fast but not hectic. It's designed for the American with limited time who wants to see everything but doesn't want the "if it's Tuesday it must be Toulouse" craziness. The route includes the predictable, "required" biggies (Eiffel Tower, Mont St. Michel, and the French Riviera) with a healthy dose of "Back Door" intimacy mixed in—a bike tour of Loire Valley châteaus, a *magnifique* castle perch from which to catch a Dordogne Valley sunset, and a touch-and-taste stroll through France's most prestigious wine caves.

This *2 to 22 Days in France* plan is shaped and balanced to avoid tourist burnout by including only the most exciting châteaus, churches, and intimate villages. We've been very selective. For example, there are beaucoup beautiful châteaus along the Loire. We'll visit the best three. The "best" is, of course, only our opinion. But after 20 busy years of travel writing, lecturing, tour guiding, and Francophilia between us, we have developed a sixth sense of what tickles the traveler's fancy in France. We love this itinerary.

Of course, fixed-route, connect-the-dots travel isn't perfect, just as color-by-numbers isn't good art. Consider this book your friendly French copilot, your Parisian in a pickle, your handbook. It's your well thought out and tested itinerary. We've done it—and refined it—many times. Use it, take advantage of it, but don't let it rule you.

Read this entire book before you go. Use it as a rack to hang more ideas on. As you plan, study, travel, and talk to people, fill the margins with notes.

This book is flexible, with 22 rearrangeable units (days) each built with these sections:

1. **Introductory Overview** for the day.
2. An hour-by-hour **Suggested Schedule** for the day.
3. A list of the most important **Sightseeing Highlights**, rated: ▲▲▲ Don't miss; ▲▲ Try hard to see; ▲ Worthwhile if you can make it; No star—Can be skipped but worth knowing about.
4. **Transportation** tips and instructions, by car and by train.
5. **Food and Accommodations:** how and where to find the best budget places, including addresses, phone numbers, general price ranges, and my favorites.
6. **Orientation** and easy-to-read **maps** locating all recommended places.

7. **Helpful Hints** on shopping, transportation, and day-to-day chores.

8. **Itinerary Options** for those with more or less than the suggested time or with particular interests. This itinerary is rubbery!

Costs, Franc-ly Speaking (6 francs = about US$1)
In spite of the topsy-turvy dollar, you can still thrive in France on $50 a day plus transportation costs. Even Paris is surprisingly affordable. Tips on budget sleeping, eating, and transportation later in this chapter give you important skills.

Your trip costs break down like this: a basic round-trip U.S.A.–Paris flight costs from $600 to $900 depending on where you fly from and when. You can sometimes save big bucks by flying into other airports and catching the train to Paris. London and Amsterdam are each about seven hours and $70 from Paris by train.

Drivers should plan on about $1,000 for a three-week car rental: car $600, gas $300, and autoroute tolls $100. Split these costs between as many people as you can jam in your car; driving with three or more gets downright cheap. To do this 22-day trip by train, you'll pay around $350.

For room and food, figure $45 a day per person, double occupancy—or $945 for three weeks. If necessary, you can travel cheaper—picnic, avoid hotel rooms equipped with bathrooms, stick to youth hostels, and so on. (See Rick Steves's *Europe Through the Back Door*, also published by John Muir Publications, for the skills and tricks of budget travel.) Add around $400 sightseeing and fun money and you've got yourself a fabulous French vacation for about $2,300.

This Book's Price Rating System
Since exact prices are impossible to predict, most prices in this book are given according to the following general ratings.

Accommodations: 1992 price for a double room, breakfast not included:

cheap	*inexpensive*	*moderate*	*expensive*
under $25	$25-$40	$40-$55	over $55
(130F)	(130-200F)	(200-280F)	(280F+)

These prices are for peak season without breakfast (usually 20F, or $4, per person extra) and, except for cheap listings, with a private shower. Hotels generally offer a wide price range, so a "moderate" hotel normally has a few "inexpensive" rooms without a bath or shower and a few "expensive" rooms with a W.C. and bath. Remember, "expensive" in this book is "budget" in most other guidebooks.

Restaurants: 1992 price for a three-course meal, drinks not included:

cheap	*inexpensive*	*moderate*	*expensive*
under $10	$10-$14	$14-$20	over $20
(50F)	(50-70F)	(70-100F)	(100F+)

The ratings are based on the cost of a fixed-price menu. Offered by most restaurants, these are generally three- or four-course meals (choice of soup, appetizer, or salad, choice of three or four entrées with vegetables, cheese course, choice of desserts), service included, but wine or drinks are not included. Again, a "moderate" restaurant may have "inexpensive" entrées for those interested in light, cheaper meals and "expensive" meals if you order high on the menu. Soft drinks and beer cost from 6F to 15F ($1-$3), and a bottle of good house wine costs from 30F to 65F ($5-$10). Free tap water is always available. Service is nearly always included in the price listed on the menu; if not, they will add it to your bill.

Admission to Sights
Approximate prices are given. While discounts are not listed, seniors (60 and over), students (with International Student Identity Cards), and youths (under 18) usually get 50 percent discounts—but only by asking.

Prices, hours, and telephone numbers are accurate as of late 1991. France is always changing, and we've tossed timidity out the window knowing you'll understand that this, like any other guidebook, starts to yellow even before it's printed.

Accommodations

One of France's great travel values, accommodations are inexpensive and a breeze to find once you've gotten the knack. You have a wide range of budget accommodations to choose from—youth hostels, campgrounds, bed and breakfasts, and one- or two-star hotels. We like places that are clean, small, central, traditional, inexpensive, not in other guidebooks, and friendly. Most places listed have at least five of these seven virtues.

Hotels: Hotel prices are for two people in a double room. Those listed in this book will range from 100F ($20, very simple, toilet and shower down the hall) to 350F ($70, maximum plumbing and more) for a double, with most clustering around 240F. Rates are higher in Paris and in other cities that are popular with tourists. A triple and a double are often the same room, with a small double bed and a sliver single, so a third person sleeps very cheaply. While groups sleep cheap, traveling alone can be expensive—the cost of a single room is usually about the same as a double.

The French have a simple hotel rating system (0 to 4 stars) depending on the amenities offered. You'll never need more than a one- or two-star hotel—trust me. More than two stars means you're paying for amenities like the availability of room service and a minibar and TV in your room. Prices vary tremendously for different rooms in the same hotel. Study the room price list posted at the desk. Understand it. Receptionists are often reluctant to even mention the cheaper rooms. You'll save about $15 on the average if you ask for a room *sans douche* (without shower, rather than *avec douche*, with shower) and just use the public shower down the hall. (In many cases, however, the rooms with baths are larger and more pleasant.) If you're on a tight budget, be sure to clarify that you don't want a bathroom; the French assume that Americans can't live without one. A bathtub (*salle de bain*) costs about $5 more than a shower (*salle d'eau*). A double bed (*grand lit*) is about $5 cheaper than twins.

Unclassified hotels (no stars) can be great bargains, though some seem to specialize in beds designed for spineless humans. Lay before you pay. You'll almost always have the option of breakfast at your hotel—pleasant and convenient, but I don't consider 30F for coffee and a croissant a good deal. Head down to the corner café, where you can break bread with the locals for half that price. In places where demand exceeds supply, many French hotels require their summertime guests to take half-pension, that is, breakfast and either lunch or dinner. It adds around 100F per person and is often a bad value. The yellow *logis de France* sign posted at the door indicates a particularly good value.

France is littered with sterile, ultra-modern, inexpensive, prefab automated hotels located usually on cheap land just outside of town. The antiseptically clean Formula 1 chain is most popular. While far from quaint, these can be a fine value (130F per room for up to three people).

Rooms are safe. Still, keep cameras and money out of sight. If that French Lincoln log pillow isn't your idea of comfort, American-style pillows are usually in the closet or available on request (say, *un oreiller, s'il vous plaît*— "un oar-ray-yeah, see-voo-play"). Remember, in Europe towels aren't routinely replaced every day; drip-dry and conserve.

To reserve a hotel room from the United States, write (simple English is usually fine) to the address listed (add the zip code found in Practical Extras) and identify clearly the dates you intend to be there. (A two-night stay in August would be "2 nuits, 16/8/91 to 18/8/91"— European hotel jargon uses your day of departure.) You will receive a letter back requesting one night's deposit. Send a $50 signed traveler's check or a bank draft in francs. Credit cards aren't usually accepted as a deposit.

You can do this tour without making long-distance hotel reservations, though I'd plan ahead for Paris at any time and for the Riviera in July and August. Even so, when you know where you'll be the next night, life on the road is easier if you telephone ahead to reserve a bed. If you phone, most hotels listed will hold a room until 18:00 with no deposit and will be accustomed to non-French speakers. Use the telephone! (Note the sample reserve-a-room-by-phone conversation in Practical Extras.) If you're unable to make it, please call and cancel your reservation.

Chambre d'Hôte (Bed and Breakfast): French chambres d'hôte (CHs), like British B&Bs, offer double the cultural intimacy for less cost than most hotels. You'll find them mainly in smaller towns and in the country-side. CHs are listed by the owner's family name. While some CHs post small Chambre or Chambre d'Hôte signs in their front windows, many can be found only through a tourist office. Doubles with breakfast cost around 170F (breakfast is not always included—ask). This is a great way to get beneath the surface with French locals. While your hosts will rarely speak English, they will almost always be enthusiastic and a delight to share a home with. CHs are always coming and going. Rather than give you a dated listing in this book, we recommend you pick up a listing at each town's TI (Tourist Information office).

France's Youth Hostels (Auberges de Jeunesse): For around $8, you can stay at one of France's plain, but pleasant, youth hostels. Remember to get a youth hostel card before you go. Travelers of any age are welcome as long as they don't mind dorm-style accommodations and love to meet other travelers. Cheap meals are sometimes available, and kitchen facilities are usually provided for do-it-yourselfers. Expect crowds in the summer, snoring, and lots of youth groups. Family rooms are sometimes available on request, but it's basically boys' dorms and girls' dorms. Unfortunately, you usually can't check in before 17:00 and must be out by 10:00. There is often a 23:00 curfew.

Le Camping in France: For around $4 per person per night, you can camp in France. This tour works great for campers. There must be more campgrounds per capita in France than anywhere else in Europe. In fact, almost every overnight stop has a campground within a reasonable walk or bus ride from the town center and train station. A tent and sleeping bag are all you need. The French love to holiday camp. It's a social, rather than an environmental, experience and a great way for traveling Americans to make French friends. Many campgrounds will have small grocery stores and washing machines, and some even come with discos and miniature golf. Hot showers are better at campgrounds than at many hotels. Serious campers should supplement this guidebook with the *Michelin Camping Guide*, available in most French bookstores, or the more thorough *Guide Officiel Camping/Caravaning* (Fédération Française de Camping et de Caravaning). Local tourist information offices also have camping information. See Practical Extras for a list of campgrounds along the 22-day route.

Café Culture and Cuisine Scene

The French have refined the art of fine living to a science. That means eating—long and well. Two-hour lunches, three-hour dinners, and endless hours sitting in outdoor cafés are the norm. They have a legislated 37-hour work-week and a self-imposed 35-hour eat week. The French spend much of their five annual weeks of paid vacation eating and drinking. Local cafés, cuisine, and wines become a highlight of any French adventure—sightseeing for your palate. Even if the rest of you is sleeping in cheap hotels, your tastebuds will want to go first class. You can eat well without going broke, but be careful: you're just as likely to blow a small fortune on a mediocre meal as you are to dine wonderfully for $10.

Petit Déjeuner (breakfast, pronounced "peh-tee day-zhu-nay"): Breakfast is typically café au lait (espresso with hot milk), hot chocolate, or tea, a roll with butter and marmalade, and a croissant. Don't expect much variety for breakfast, but the bread is fresh and the coffee is

great. It's cheaper and entirely acceptable to buy a croissant or roll at a nearby bakery and eat it with your coffee
at a café. If the morning egg-urge gets the best of you,
drop into a café and order *une omelette* or *oeufs sur le
plat* (fried eggs). You could also buy or bring a couple of
plastic bowls and spoons from home, buy a box of
French cereal and a small box of milk, and eat in your
room before heading out for coffee. I carry a package of
Vache Qui Rit (Laughing Cow) cheese to supplement the
morning jelly. (See the Café Culture tips below before
ordering your first breakfast out.)

Déjeuner (lunch): French picnics can be first-class
affairs. On days you choose to picnic, gather supplies
early; you'll probably visit several small stores to assemble a complete meal, and many close at noon. Look for a
boulangerie (bakery), a *crémerie* (cheeses), a *charcuterie*
(deli items, meats, and pâtés), an *épicerie* (general market
with veggies, drinks, etc.), and a *pâtisserie* (delicious pastries). Local *supermarchés* offer less color and cost, more
efficiency, and good quality. On the outskirts of cities,
you'll find appropriately named *hypermarchés*. Go into
at least one of these monsters for a glimpse of hyper
France in action.

My picnic paraphernalia includes a cardboard box for
my backseat pantry, plastic cups, paper towels, water bottle (buy a half-liter plastic bottle of Vittel mineral water
and reuse the handy screw-top container), a damp cloth
in a zip-lock baggie, a Swiss army knife, and a petite table-
cloth. French picnics are an adventure in high cuisine. Be
daring. Try the smelly cheeses, ugly pâtés, sissy quiches,
and miniscule yogurts. Local shopkeepers are happy to
sell small quantities of produce. A typical picnic for two
might be half a baguette (say *demi* and they'll cut it), two
tomatoes, three carrots, 100 grams of cheese, 100 grams
of meat (the equivalent of two Quarter Pounders), two
apples, a liter box of orange juice, and a yogurt. Total cost
is about $8.

When not in the picnicking mood, look for food
stands selling take-out sandwiches and drinks, or crêper-
ies or brasseries for fast and easy sit-down restaurant

food. Brasseries are cafés serving basic fare such as omelets, chicken, and fries as well as simple sandwiches and
salads. Many French restaurants offer good value, three-
to five-course menus at lunch only. The same menu is
often 20F more at dinner. Drivers will find plenty of roadside *frites* trailers selling fries, hot snacks, drinks, and so
on.

Dîner (dinner, pronounced "dee-nay"): This is where
the careless get creamed. When restaurant hunting,
choose places filled with locals, not places with big neon
signs boasting, We Speak English. When you're on the
road, look for the red and blue *Relais routier* decal
indicating that the place is recommended by the truckers'
union. Look for menus (*la carte*) posted outside; if you
don't see one, move along. Also look for set-price menus
(*prix fixe*, often just called *le menu*) that give you several
choices among several courses—appetizer, main dish,
dessert or cheese, sometimes wine, always service. This is
the best value when ordering a full meal. Don't hesitate to
ask a waiter for help in deciphering a menu. Go with his
recommendations and anything *de la maison*. Galloping
gourmets should bring a menu translator (the Marling
Menu Master is excellent). Remember, if you ask for a
menu, you'll get a meal; *la carte* is the list of what's cooking. The wines are often listed in a separate *carte des vins*.
Tipping (*pourboire*) is unnecessary.

Drinks: I drink the water throughout France. For a
free pitcher in a restaurant, ask for *une carafe d'eau, s il
vous plâit*. Be careful, you may unwittingly buy bottled
water. (*L'eau du robinet* is tap water in French.) Wine-
wise, you could drink your budget into oblivion if you're
not careful. The most famous wines are the most expensive, while less-known taste-alikes remain a bargain (see
my regional suggestions for ideas). If you like brandy, try
Armagnac, Cognac's cheaper twin brother. France's best
beer is Alsatian; try Krönenburg or the heavier Pelfort.
For a fun, bright, nonalcoholic drink, order *un diabolo
menthe* (7-Up with mint syrup). You won't find many diet
drinks in France, and ice cubes are rare.

Here are a few budget tips. In stores, unrefrigerated soft

drinks and beer are a third the price of cold drinks. Avoid buying drinks to go at street-side stands; you'll find them far cheaper at a market. When ordering a beer at a café or restaurant, ask for *une pression* (draft beer), which is cheaper than bottled. When ordering table wine at a café or restaurant, ask for *un picket* (a pitcher), again cheaper than a bottle. If all you want is a glass of wine, ask for *une verre de vin*. Try to keep a water bottle with you. Water quenches your thirst better and cheaper than anything you'll find in a store or café.

Café Culture: French cafés provide refuge from museum and church overload and are ideal spots from which to watch the river of France flow by. Put on a beret and shades and get into some of Europe's best people-watching. Caution: French cafés charge different prices for the same drink depending on where you sit. Check the posted price list before ordering. You'll see two price columns, *comptoir* (counter) and the more expensive *salle* (seated). The outdoor tables are most expensive and scenic. Don't hesitate to sip at the counter, it's cheaper—often half the price of the salle. Cafés on squares and grand boulevards are much more expensive than the smaller cafés on small streets.

Car Rental
Research car rentals before you go. It's much cheaper to arrange car rentals in the United States, so check rates with your travel agent. Leasing, which is tax-free (saving about 28 percent in France) and cheaper than long-term renting, requires a minimum three-week contract. Ask your travel agent for details. For this itinerary, plan to pick up and drop off your car in Paris, at Orly airport, in Versailles, or in Rouen. I normally rent the smallest, least expensive model, such as a Renault-5 or Ford Fiesta.

Driving in France
The hardest thing about driving in France, outside Paris, is not stopping at every mouth-watering bakery and pâtisserie you pass. All you need is your valid U.S. driver's license and a car. International driver's licenses are not

necessary. Seat belts are mandatory, and children under ten must be in the back seat.

Gas is expensive: figure about $4 per gallon. It's most expensive on autoroutes and 10 percent cheaper at supermarkets (a $4 savings per tank). Autoroute tolls may shock you; four hours of travel costs about $15. But the alternative to these super "feeways" is often being marooned in rural traffic. Autoroutes usually save enough time, gas, and nausea to justify the splurge. Mix scenic country road rambling with high-speed "autorouting," but don't forget that in France, the shortest line between almost any two points is the autoroute. Driving the entire 22-day tour on autoroutes whenever available would cost a total of about $100.

Roads in France are classified into Departmental (D), National (N), and Autoroutes (A). D routes (usually yellow lines on maps) are slow and often the most scenic. N routes (usually red lines) can be as fast as the autoroutes (orange lines). Green road signs are for national routes, blue for autoroutes. There are plenty of good facilities, gas stations, and rest stops along all French roads. Lead-free gas (*sans plomb*) is becoming quite common.

Here are a few French road tips. In city centers, traffic merging from the right normally has the right of way, *priorité à droite*. Approach intersections cautiously. When navigating through cities, stow the map and follow the signs—*Centre-ville* (downtown) and from there to the tourist information office. When leaving (or just passing through), follow the *Toutes Directions* or *Autres Directions* (meaning anywhere else) signs until you see a sign for your specific destination. Be careful of sluggish tractors on country roads. From 12:00 to 14:00, while the French are eating and many sights are closed, you can make great time driving. The French drive fast and tailgate.

Parking is a headache in the larger cities. Pay to park at well-patrolled lots or use the parking meters, which are free from 12:00 to 14:00 and after 19:00 until 9:00. Tourists are rarely given parking tickets. You might want to keep a pile of 1F and 2F coins in your ashtray for parking meters, public phones, and laundromat dryers.

France by Train

This tour is designed for both car and train travel.
France's rail system (SNCF) is Europe's best and a bargain.
Take advantage of the railpasses offered. While Eurail-
passes work well (one offers three weeks of unlimited
first-class travel in 17 European countries, including
France, for $550, another gives you any 14 days of travel
out of 30 for $610), those traveling solely within France
will save the most money with a Francerail pass (available
outside of France only, through your travel agent). For
this 22-day tour (which requires only 13 train travel days),
buy the Francerail pass that is valid for one month and
can be used any 9 days in that month (about $230 second
class, about $330 first class) and buy tickets as you go for
the extra days. The Francerail pass includes a two-day
Paris subway and bus pass as well as free transportation
from the airport into Paris.

Train travel in France is ideal for solo travelers. It's
cheaper than car rental, and you'll make plenty of rail
friends. Train stations are almost always centrally located
in cities, making hotel hunting and sightseeing easier.
Since train travel is less flexible than car travel, I've prepared some separate daily schedules for itineraries "by
car" and "by train." I've also listed local bus schedules
and good rental bike routes for sightseeing. Verify every
schedule shown in this book ahead of time to avoid
unhappy surprises. Reservations are generally unnecessary except for the 170 mph TGV trains. Railpass holders
also need reservations for these "bullet trains"; they're
cheap and easy to get at the station. Validate (*composter*)
all train tickets and reservations in the orange machines
located before the platforms. (Watch others and repeat.)
For more information on rail-riding skills, read *Europe
Through the Back Door* (see Recommended Guidebooks,
below).

Train and Car Combo

The French railroad, SNCF, offers a car/train combination
package. For a reasonable price, couples can ride the train
or use a rental car for any 15 days out of 30. The possibili-

ties are endless. Ask your travel agent for details on this
wonderfully flexible new transportation pass.

Biking in France

Throughout France you'll find areas where public transportation is limited and bicycle touring is an excellent
idea. Most French train stations rent bikes. Their fee is a
standard 55F per day and 40F per half-day. Areas where
bike touring is good usually have plenty of bike rental
places.

When to Go

Spring and fall are best. April in Paris and September in
Provence are what poets write about. Europeans vacation
in July and August, jamming the Riviera (August is worst).
While many French businesses close in August, the
traveler hardly notices it. Sights, cafés, restaurants, and
hotels are in full swing and ready to take your money.
Winter travel is okay—you'll find gray, but generally mild,
weather along most of this route. Sights and tourist information offices keep shorter hours, and some tourist
activities (like English-language castle tours) vanish
altogether.

Francophobia and the Language Barrier

You've no doubt heard that "the French are mean and
cold and refuse to speak English." This image comes from
Parisians only. The French do tend to take great pride in
their culture, clinging to their belief in cultural superi-
ority despite the fact that they're no longer a world super-
power. Let's face it, it's tough to keep on smiling when
you've been crushed by a Big Mac, lashed by Levis, and
drowned in instant coffee. The French are cold only if
you decide to see them that way. Look for friendliness,
and give them the benefit of the doubt. Remember, they
take their culture and croissants seriously. The fine points
of culture, not rugged Yankee individualism, are respected here.

Communication difficulties in France are exaggerated.
While it's true that you won't find many French people

who are fluent in English, the French speak much better English than we Americans speak French. To hurdle the language barrier, bring a phrase book, a menu reader, and a good supply of patience. If you learn only four phrases, learn and use these: *bonjour* (good day), *merçi* (thank you), *pardon* (pardon me), and *s'il vous plâit* (please). The French place great importance on politeness; they're only rude to rude people.

The French are language perfectionists—they take their language, and other languages, seriously. Often they speak more English than they let on. This isn't a tourist-baiting tactic but timidity on their part to speak another language less than fluently. Start any conversation with "Bonjour Madame/ Monsieur, parlez-vous anglais?" and hope they speak more English than you speak French. Even if they don't, this greases the skids for any help you may need. Learn the essential phrases, especially the polite words.

Stranger in a Strange Land

We travel all the way to France to enjoy differences—to become temporary locals. You'll experience frustrations. Certain truths that we find "God-given" or "self-evident," like cold beer, ice, a bottomless cup of coffee, long, hot showers, and bigger being better, are suddenly not so true. One of the benefits of travel is the eye-opening realization that there are logical, civil, and even better, alternatives. Travel tends to pry open one's hometown blinders. If the beds are too short, the real problem is that you are too long. Don't look for things American on the other side of the Atlantic and you're sure to enjoy a good deal of French hospitality. *Vive la différence!*

Tourist Information Offices (TIs)

The French call their tourist offices Syndicat d'Initiative, Office de Tourisme, Bureau de Tourisme, or Information Touristique. To add to the confusion, I'll refer to them from now on as "TIs" (for "Tourist Information"). TIs in France are everywhere and are usually well organized, English-speaking, and closed from 12:00 to 14:00. Most

will help you find a room and will call hotels for you (for
a small fee). The TI should be your first stop in any new
city. Try to arrive, or at least telephone, before they close.
They often organize regional tours and have the most
complete listings of bed and breakfasts available.

Travel Smart
Lay your departure groundwork upon arrival in a town.
Read a day ahead in this book, use the local tourist
offices, and enjoy the Gallic friendliness of the local people. Don't be afraid to ask questions. Most locals are eager
to point you in their idea of the right direction and tell
you about their town's history. Use the telephone, wear
your money belt, and use a small pocket notepad to
organize your thoughts. Make simplicity a virtue. Those
who expect to travel smart, do.
    Pace yourself. The overall plan and each daily schedule
are very carefully laid out. However, each traveler's touring tempo is different, and you'll want to personalize this
busy schedule, plugging in rest days and skipping some
sights where and when you need to. Read through this
itinerary and decide for yourself where you want to
spend more or less time. Play with the calendar and try to
plan your schedule to avoid arriving at important sights
on closed days or at peak times. Troubleshoot problems
before you leave. Stretching this trip to 28 or 30 days
would be ideal. I've worked to minimize one-night
stands. So should you.

Red Tape, Business Hours, Banking, and Francs
You currently need a passport but no visa and no shots to
travel in France.
    In France—and in this book—you'll be using the
24-hour clock (also known as military time). After 12:00
noon, just keep going. Instead of 1:00 p.m., you'll see
13:00, 14:00 (for 2:00 p.m.), and so on (just subtract 12
and add p.m.).
    This book lists most of the on- and off-season hours of
France's sightseeing attractions. In off-season, expect
generally shorter hours and more lunchtime breaks.

Much of France shuts down from 12:00 to 14:00. Lunch is sacred. On Mondays, many businesses are closed at least until 14:00 and often all day. Many small markets, boulangeries, and the like, are open Sunday mornings until 12:00. Beware: many sights stop admitting people 30 minutes before they close.

Banking hours vary, though most banks are open from 9:00 to 16:30 on weekdays. Main offices often remain open Saturday mornings until 12:00, and many are closed Mondays. Shop around for the best exchange rate and lowest commission. Some banks charge no commission, others charge up to $4. The best exchange rates are often accompanied by the highest commissions.

PTT means postal, telegraph, and telephone service in France. Post offices are open 8:00 to 19:00 weekdays and 8:00 to 12:00 on Saturdays. (PTTs in smaller towns close for lunch, 12:00-14:00.) If you know what stamps you need, you can buy them more easily at a *tabac* (tobacconist's shop).

To arrange for mail delivery in France, either reserve a few hotels along your route in advance and give their addresses to friends or use American Express Mail Services. Any American Express office in France will keep mail addressed to you for one month. Pick up a list of overseas offices at any U.S. American Express agency. This service is free to anyone using an AmExCo card or traveler's checks and available to others for a small fee.

The French franc is divided into 100 centimes. Learn to recognize the larger coins: ½ F, 1F, 2F, 5F, and 10F. Currency comes in 20F, 50F, 100F, 200F, and 500F denominations. There are about 6 francs in a U.S. dollar.

Carry your money in traveler's checks and spend French cash.

The French arrange dates by day/month/year, so Christmas would be 25-12-91. What we Americans call the second floor of a building is the first floor in France. Commas and periods are often switched, so there are 5.280 feet in a mile, and if your temperature is more than 98,6 degrees, you've got a fever.

Telephones

You can usually make long-distance phone calls from PTTs, but you'll pay more and wait longer than if you use the public phones on the street.

A super-efficient, vandal-resistant card-operated system is rapidly replacing France's coin-operated public phone system. You'll still find the soon-to-be-extinct coin phones in smaller cities. The coin phones are self-explanatory, usually with English instructions for international calls. To call the United States, drop in a 5F coin, dial 19-1-area code-number and you're in business, for 20 seconds anyway.

The coin-free card system is even easier. Buy a phone card (Télécarte in French), available at any PTT, tourist office, SNCF station, and most tabacs. The smallest value is 40F. The price of the call, local or international, will automatically be deducted from the card. To use the card-phone booths, follow the instructions that, in French, will prompt you to (1) pick up the receiver; (2) insert the card; (3) close the lid over the card; (4) wait a few seconds; and (5) dial your number. Buy a card at the beginning of your trip and use it for hotel reservations, tourist information, and phoning home.

From Paris you must dial 16 to get a long-distance line for calls within France. To dial Paris from elsewhere in France, you must dial 16-1, then the eight-digit number. To and from all other cities, simply dial the eight-digit number listed.

Recommended Guidebooks

While many will have a great trip relying solely on this book, you may want some supplemental travel information, especially if you expect to deviate from this 22-day plan. When you consider the improvements they'll make in your $2,000 vacation, $25 or $35 for extra maps and books is money well spent. In France, one decent budget tip can easily save the price of an extra guidebook.

Let's Go: France (New York: St. Martin's Press, annual) is the best general guide to sights, hotels, and restaurants in France. Highly opinionated and student oriented, this guide is best for young train travelers on a tight budget. But even if you're rich and driving, it's a good investment.

The popular, skinny, green Michelin Guides are excellent, especially if you're driving. They are known for their city and sightseeing maps, dry but concise and helpful information on all major sights, and good cultural and historical background. They cost $12 in the United States, much less in France. English editions are available for these parts of the 22-day plan: Paris, Provence, the Loire, Côte d'Azur (Riviera), Normandy, and the Dordogne. They are easy to pick up as you go but sometimes tough to find in English.

There are many other guidebooks on France and Paris. Most are high on facts and low on opinion, guts, or personality. For an excellent catalog of available guidebooks, call Book Passage in California at 1-800-321-9785.

Rick Steves's Books: Finally, I've written this book assuming that you've read or will read the latest editions of my books *Europe Through the Back Door* (Santa Fe, N.M.: John Muir Publications, 1990) and *Europe 101: History and Art for the Traveler* (Santa Fe, N.M.: John Muir Publications, 1990). They provide the foundation of travel skills and history and art background on which to build your trip.

Europe Through the Back Door gives you the basic skills that make this demanding 22-day plan possible. Chapters cover minimizing jet lag, packing light, driving or train travel, finding budget beds without reservations, changing money, theft, terrorism, hurdling the language barrier, health, travel photography, ugly-Americanism, laundry, itinerary strategies, and more. The book also includes special articles on my 40 favorite "Back Doors."

Europe 101: History and Art for the Traveler (co-written with Gene Openshaw) gives you the story of Europe's people, history, and art. A little "101" background knowledge really helps France's sights come alive.

My newest book, *Mona Winks* (Santa Fe, N.M.: John Muir Publications, 1988), also co-written with Gene Openshaw, gives you fun, easy-to-follow self-guided tours of Europe's top 20 museums, including the Louvre, the Orsay Museum, the Pompidou Modern Art Museum in Paris, and the Palace of Versailles.

To update this book before you fly and to share travel tips, have your computer call Rick Steves's free computer bulletin board travel information service at 206/771-1902, any time.

Maps: Don't skimp on maps. Excellent Michelin maps are available at good bookstores in the United States and (cheaper) throughout France in bookstores, newsstands, and gas stations. Train travelers can do fine with Michelin's #989 France map (1/1,000,000) and an occasional regional map (1/200,000). Drivers should buy the soft cover Michelin France atlas (the entire country at 1/200,000, well organized in a book with an index and maps of major cities, available all over France for about $20). Study and learn the Michelin key to get the most sightseeing value out of their maps. The maps in this book, drawn by Dave Hoerlein, are concise and simple. Dave, who has traveled the 22-day route, has designed the maps to make the text easier to follow. They will help you locate recommended places and get to the tourist offices, where you'll find more in-depth maps (usually free) of the cities or regions.

Raise Your Travel Dreams to Their Upright and Locked Position

Our goal is to free you, not chain you. Please defend your spontaneity as you would your mother. Use this book to avoid time- and money-wasting mistakes, to get more intimate with France by traveling as a temporary local person, and as a starting point from which to shape your best possible travel experience.

Be confident. Enjoy the hills as well as the valleys. Judging from all the positive feedback and happy postcards I receive from travelers who have used these "2 to 22 Days" guidebooks, it's safe to assume you're on your way to a great French vacation—independent, inexpensive, and with the finesse of an experienced traveler. Bon voyage!

AS TAUGHT IN *EUROPE THROUGH THE BACK DOOR*

Travel is intensified living—maximum thrills per minute and one of the last great sources of legal adventure. Travel is freedom. It's recess, and we need it.

Experiencing the real Europe requires catching it by surprise, going casual...."Through the Back Door."

Affording travel is a matter of priorities. (Make do with the old car.) You can travel—simple, safe, and comfortable—anywhere in Europe for $50 a day plus transportation costs. In many ways, spending more money only builds a thicker wall between you and what you came to see. Europe is a cultural carnival, and time after time, you'll find that its best acts are free and the best seats are the cheap ones.

A tight budget forces you to travel close to the ground, meeting and communicating with the people, not relying on service with a purchased smile. Never sacrifice sleep, nutrition, safety, or cleanliness in the name of budget. Simply enjoy the local-style alternatives to expensive hotels and restaurants.

Extroverts have more fun. If your trip is low on magic moments, kick yourself and make things happen. If you don't enjoy a place, maybe you don't know enough about it. Seek the truth. Recognize tourist traps. Give a people the benefit of your open mind. See things as different but not better or worse. Any culture has much to share.

Of course, travel, like the world, is a series of hills and valleys. Be fanatically positive and militantly optimistic. If something's not to your liking, change your liking. Travel is addicting. It can make you a happier American, as well as a citizen of the world. Our Earth is home to six billion equally important people. It's humbling to travel and find that people don't envy Americans. They like us, but with all due respect, they wouldn't trade places.

Globe-trotting destroys ethnocentricity. It helps you understand and appreciate different cultures. Travel changes people. It broadens perspectives and teaches new ways to measure quality of life. Many travelers toss aside their hometown blinders. Their prized souvenirs are the strands of different cultures they decide to knit into their own character. The world is a cultural yarn shop. And Back Door Travelers are weaving the ultimate tapestry. Come on, raise your travel dreams to their upright and locked position, and join in!

DAY 1   Your French adventure begins in France's capital and most beautiful city, Paris. Leave your bag and jet lag at your hotel and take a get-to-know-Paris stroll.

DAYS 2 and 3   Parisian highlights fill these two busy days. Climb Notre Dame and the Eiffel Tower, cruise the Seine and Champs-Elysées, and master the Louvre and Orsay museums. Save some after-dark energy for one of the world's most romantic cities.

DAY 4   Spend your morning visiting Europe's palace of palaces, Versailles. There's still much more to Paris. How about a stroll through Paris's most interesting ex-marsh, Le Marais, or some modern art at the razzle-dazzle Pompidou Center, or space age shopping at Les Halles?

DAY 5   Start using your train pass or pick up your rental car and follow the Seine west to Normandy. Spend the day in historic Rouen surrounded by half-timbered houses, Gothic spires, and fiery memories of Joan of Arc. You'll bed down in a nearby fishing village with more charm than fish.

DAY 6   Today it's a hop, skip, and jump from the Battle of Hastings to the battlefields of D day to the wondrous Mont St. Michel. Your day's finale is a nighttime stroll around Mont St. Michel, one of Europe's great experiences.

DAY 7   After touring Mont St. Michel inside and out, sample Brittany's top city and tastiest crêpes before zipping to château heaven, the Loire Valley. Your destination, Amboise, huddles on the Loire River underneath its cliff-hanging château. Leonardo da Vinci spent his last years here; you have two nights.

DAY 8   Today is for château lovers. You'll bike, drive, or bus to the most exciting château in the Loire Valley. This beautiful area was made for biking, and you're probably ready for a break from the car or train. You can ride short or long. The cycling options are endless.

DAY 9   It's due south into the heart and kitchen of France. Scenery, food, and castles don't come any better. Your home tonight is a feudal fantasy—the city of Sarlat.

DAY 10   Today you'll see the last great ancient (15,000 years old) cave paintings still open to the public. The afternoon is yours to explore a few of the 1,000 castles and rock-sculpted villages that dot France's beautiful Dordogne Valley.

DAY 11   You'll visit three of Europe's medieval all-stars today—the three-towered bridge in Cahors, the fortified church in Albi, and the magnificent medieval fortress city of Carcassonne.

DAY 12   Scamper up the ramparts and walk the time-stained walls of Carcassonne. After lunch, cut across southern France to establish a home base where van Gogh did, in Arles. An early afternoon and evening here will give you time to find the light, ambience, and color-ful corners that so inspired Vincent.

DAY 13   Today is devoted to sampling the cities and scenery of Provence. Breakfast high in the ghost town of Les Baux, lunch on France's greatest Roman remnant, the Pont du Gard, and enjoy an afternoon in Avignon, the city the popes once dumped Rome for.

DAYS 14 and 15   Ah, how about a sunny vacation from your vacation? Set up beach camp in Nice and recharge your sightseeing batteries. This is your fun in the sun stop. Nearby Antibes has fine beaches, Monte Carlo welcomes all with open cash registers, hill towns offer a breezy and photogenic alternative to the beach scene, and the entire area is speckled with avant-garde art galleries. Evenings on the Riviera were made for the promenade. Join the parade or at least grab a good seat and watch.

DAY 16   Trade Riviera palm trees for Alpine snowballs today as you surround yourself with Europe's highest peaks in Chamonix. The trip is long, the scenery spectacular.

DAY 17   This is Alps admiration day. Take Europe's ultimate cable car ride up and over the 12,600-foot Aiguille du Midi past Mont Blanc to the Italian border. Spend the afternoon recovering from the morning's high-wire drama on a pleasant hike.

DAY 18   Coast down the Alps into Burgundy to set up in Beaune, France's prestigious wine capital. Tonight you'll savor the wine, food, and view from a hilltop restaurant.

DAY 19   Start today touring a remarkable fifteenth-century hospital. Enjoy a picnic lunch in front of our favorite French castle and end the day at the world's only wine smorgasbord, learning why, when you say fine wine, so many people think Burgundy. You'll dine in the vineyards this evening.

DAY 20   After a backdoor walking tour through the world's mustard capital, Dijon, head north to Alsace, where France blends into Germany. If you've been dying to try out your German, now's your chance. Home base is Colmar, a lovable mix of the best of French and German cultures, where they serve sauerkraut with fine sauces.

DAY 21   After a morning exploring Colmar's fine pedestrian streets and powerful Unterlinden Museum, wander Alsace's *Route du Vin*—storks, cute villages, endless vineyards, and peace.

DAY 22 Break today's long haul with stops at the World War I battlefields of Verdun, where over 1,000,000 men made the "ultimate sacrifice," and Reims for a look at its grand Gothic cathedral and a champagne tour. You'll arrive back home in Paris in time for a nostalgic walk and a farewell dinner.

Regions of France

ARRIVE IN PARIS

What a way to start a tour! Paris offers sweeping boulevards, sleepy parks, world-class art galleries, chatty crêpe stands, Napoleon's body, sleek shopping malls, the Eiffel Tower, and people-watching from outdoor cafés. Many people fall in love with Paris. Some see the essentials and flee, overwhelmed by the huge city. With the proper approach and a good orientation, you'll fall head over heels for Europe's capital city.

However you arrive, today's goal is to get comfortably set up in your hotel, learn the subway system, and take a bonjour Paris orientation walk through the city's old core. The next few pages are vital for a quick understanding of this exciting city.

Airport Strategy

Both of Paris's efficient international airports have good public transportation into the city and offer handy, uncrowded tourist information services. After clearing customs, visit the tourist office (tel. 48 62 22 80) behind the "meeting point" at Charles de Gaulle. At Orly, get information at the ADP counter (Paris airport services, tel. 49 75 15 15) near Gate H. Pick up sightseeing and events information and two free city maps (tear the subway map out of one for your shirt pocket). Ask where you can buy a phone card (télécarte). Call to confirm hotel reservations or find a room. Be sure to get the Métro stop nearest to your hotel. If you're having trouble, the tourist office or ADP can help.

Getting into Paris: From Charles de Gaulle, catch the free shuttle bus (called *navette*, gate 28) to Roissy Rail, where a train will zip you into the heart of Paris's subway system (29F, free with a railpass; follow the flow, 90% of the crowd is going into Paris).

To get from Charles de Gaulle to hotels in the recommended rue Cler area, take the Air France bus (40F) to the Arc de Triomphe. Cross ave. Carnot to ave. MacMahon, catch the #92 bus in the direction of Arc de Triomphe (stop is right in front of you) and ride to Bosquet and St. Dominique stop.

From Orly, several rail or bus options can take you to different parts of the city. Orly-rail runs every 15 minutes direct from Orly (near baggage claim) into the Paris Métro system for 25F. The Air France bus (36F) at Gate H will take you to Les Invalides Métro station (near rue Cler). Taxis are expensive (150F from Orly, 200F from Charles de Gaulle).

Train Station Strategy
Paris has six train stations, all with Métro connections and most with tourist information offices. If you're coming from northern or central Europe, you'll land at the Gare de l'Est, Gare du Nord, or Gare St. Lazare. From the south, you arrive at the Austerlitz or Lyon station. Pick up the RATP Métro and bus map and use the phones (télécartes are sold at any ticket window) to find a hotel. Follow signs to the Métro; study the map and the instructions below before plunging into the system.

Paris Orientation
Paris is circled by a ring road freeway (the *périphérique*), split in half by the Seine River, and divided into 20 *arrondissements* (proud and independent governmental jurisdictions). You'll find Paris much easier to negotiate if you know which side of the river you're on, which arrondissement you're in, and which subway (métro) stop you're closest to. Remember, if you're above the river (look at a map), you're on the right bank (*rive droite*), and if you're below it, you're on the left bank (*rive gauche*). Arrondissements are numbered, starting at ground zero (Notre-Dame is 1ème) and moving in a clockwise spiral out to the ring road. The last two digits in a Parisian zip code are the arrondissement number, and the notation for the métro stop is "Mo." In Parisian jargon, Napoleon's tomb is on la rive gauche in the "7ème," zip code 75007, Métro: Invalides. Paris métro stops are a standard aid in giving directions.

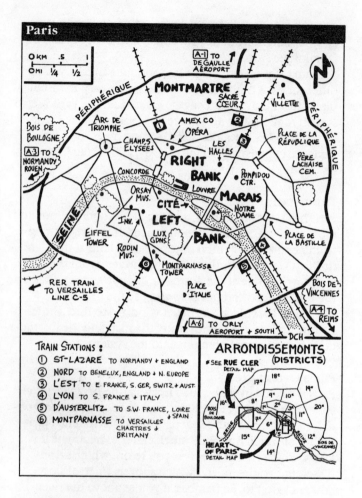

Paris

0 KM .5 1
0 MI ¼ ½

A-1 TO DE GAULLE AÉROPORT

MONTMARTRE
SACRÉ CŒUR
LA VILLETTE

PÉRIPHÉRIQUE

ARC DE TRIOMPHE
BOIS DE BOULOGNE
A-3 TO NORMANDY ROUEN

AMEX CO
OPÉRA ①
②
③
PLACE DE LA RÉPUBLIQUE

CHAMPS ELYSÉES
LES HALLES
PÈRE LACHAISE CEM.

CONCORDE
RIGHT BANK
POMPIDOU CTR.

ORSAY MUS.
LOUVRE
MARAIS

CITÉ
NOTRE DAME

SEINE
INV.
LEFT
LUX GDNS.
BANK
④
PLACE DE LA BASTILLE

EIFFEL TOWER
RODIN MUS.
⑥
MONTPARNASSE TOWER
⑤

RER TRAIN TO VERSAILLES LINE C-5

PLACE D'ITALIE
BOIS DE VINCENNES

A-6 TO ORLY AEROPORT & SOUTH
A-4 TO REIMS

DCH

TRAIN STATIONS :
① ST-LAZARE TO NORMANDY & ENGLAND
② NORD TO BENELUX, ENGLAND & N. EUROPE
③ L'EST TO E. FRANCE, S. GER, SWITZ. & AUST.
④ LYON TO S. FRANCE & ITALY
⑤ D'AUSTERLITZ TO S.W. FRANCE, LOIRE & SPAIN
⑥ MONTPARNASSE TO VERSAILLES, CHARTRES & BRITTANY

ARRONDISSEMONTS (DISTRICTS)

SEE RUE CLER DETAIL MAP

18ᵉ
17ᵉ
16ᵉ
BOIS DE BOULOGNE
8ᵉ 9ᵉ 10ᵉ 19ᵉ
2ᵉ 3ᵉ
1ᵉʳ
7ᵉ
SEINE
6ᵉ 5ᵉ
15ᵉ
"HEART OF PARIS" DETAIL MAP
14ᵉ
13ᵉ
12ᵉ
11ᵉ
20ᵉ
SEINE
BOIS DE VINCENNES

Parisian Public Transit

The Métro: Europe's best subway is divided into two
systems; the métro covers the city and the RER connects
suburban destinations. You'll be using the métro for
almost all your trips. In Paris, you're never more than a
ten-minute walk from a métro station. One ticket takes
you anywhere in the system with unlimited transfers.
Save nearly 50 percent by buying a *carnet* (pronounced
car-nay) of 10 tickets for about 35F at any métro station.
Métro tickets work on city buses. If you're staying longer

the *Carte d'Orange* gives you free run of the métro and buses from Sunday through Saturday for 51F.

Before entering the station, find the "Mo." stop closest to your destination and which line(s) will get you there. The lines have numbers, but they're best known by their *direction* or end-of-the-line stop. (For example, the Saint-Denis/Châtillon line runs between Saint-Denis in the north and Châtillon in the south.)

Once in the métro station, you'll see signs directing you to the train going in your direction (e.g., direction: Saint-Denis). Insert your ticket in the automatic turnstile (brown stripe down), pass through the turnstile, reclaim and keep your ticket until you exit the system (toss it out when done so you don't confuse old and new tickets). Transfers are free and can be made wherever lines cross. When you transfer, look for the orange *correspondance* (connections) signs when you exit your first train, then follow the proper "direction" or "destination" sign.

Before you *sortie* (that's exit, not bomb), check the very helpful *plan du quartier* (map of the neighborhood) to get your bearings and decide which sortie you want. At stops with several sorties, you can save lots of walking by choosing the best exit. Remember your essential métro words: *direction* (direction), *correspondance* (connections), *sortie* (exit), *carnet* (cheap set of 10 tickets), and *"Donnez-moi mon porte-monnaie!"* (Give me back my wallet.) Thieves thrive in the métro. Keep valuables in your money belt.

The RER suburban train system (thick lines on your map) works like the métro—but much speedier because it makes only a few stops within the city. One métro ticket is all you need for RER rides within Paris. To travel outside the city (to Versailles, for example), you'll need to buy another ticket at the station window. Save lots of time by using the RER whenever you can.

Public Buses: The trickier bus system is worth figuring out and using. The same yellow tickets are good on both bus and métro, though you can't use the same ticket to transfer between the two systems, and longer rides require more than one ticket. While the métro shuts

down about 00:45, some buses continue much later.
Schedules are posted at bus stops.

To ride the bus, study the big system maps at each stop
to figure out which route(s) you need. Then look at the
individual route diagrams, showing the exact route of the
lines serving that stop to verify your route. Major stops
are also painted on the side of each bus. Enter through
the front doors. Punch your yellow métro ticket in the
machine behind the driver, or pay the higher cash fare.
Get off the bus using the rear door. Even if you're not certain you've figured it out, do some joy riding (outside of
rush hour). Lines 24, 63, and 69 run Paris's most scenic
routes and make a great introduction to this city.

Taxis: Parisian taxis are nearly reasonable. A ten-
minute ride costs about 40F (versus 4F to get anywhere in
town on the métro), and luggage will cost you more. You
can try waving one down, but it's easier to ask for the
nearest taxi stand ("oo-ay la tet de stah-see-oh"). Sunday
and night rates are higher, and if you call one from your
hotel, the meter starts as soon as the call is received. Taxis
are tough to find on Friday and Saturday nights, especially after the métro closes.

Paris Information
Paris requires study and a good map. For an extended
stay, two fine guidebooks are the *Michelin Green Guide*
and the *Access Guide to Paris*. While it's easy to pick up
free maps of Paris once you've arrived (your hotel has
them), they don't show all the streets, and you may want
the huge Michelin #10 map of Paris. The *Pariscope*
weekly magazine (or one of its clones, 3F, at any news-
stand) lists museum hours, concerts and musical festivals,
plays, movies, nightclubs, and special art exhibits.

There are 11 English-language bookstores in Paris
where you can pick up guidebooks. Try Shakespeare and
Co. for used travel books (at 37 rue de la Boucherie,
across the river from Notre-Dame, 12:00-24:00) or W. H.
Smith's at 248 rue de Rivoli, or Brentanos at 47 avenue de
L'Opéra.

The American Church is a nerve center for the American émigré community and publishes a handy monthly called the *Free Voice. France-USA Contacts*, an advertisement paper, is full of useful information for those looking for work or long-term housing.

Avoid the Paris TIs—long lines and short information. This book, the *Pariscope* magazine, and a good map are all you need for a short visit. If you need more information, visit the main TI (tel. 47 23 61 72, at 127 ave. des Champs-Élysées, open 9:00-20:00), or ask your hotelier. For recorded concert and special events information in English, call 47 20 88 98. For a complete list of museum hours and scheduled English museum tours, pick up the free *Musées, Monuments Historiques, et Expositions* booklet from any museum.

Helpful Hints

Most museums are closed on Tuesday, have reduced entries on Sunday, and are least crowded very early, at lunch, and very late. Carry small change for pay toilets, or walk into any café with outdoor tables like you owned the place and find the toilet in the back. Check price lists before ordering at any café or restaurant. Rude surprises await sloppy tourists. Remember, pedestrians don't have the right of way—drivers do and they know it. Use your money belt, and never carry a wallet in your back pocket or a purse over your shoulder.

Don't try to see it all, pace yourself, enjoy the cafés between sightseeing and shopping. Assume you'll return. Useful telephone numbers: American Express, 42 66 09 99; American Hospital, 46 41 25 25; American Pharmacies at 47 42 49 40 (Opéra) and 42 60 72 96 (Tuileries); Police, 17; U.S. Embassy, 42 96 12 02; Paris and France directory assistance, 12; ATT operator 19 00 11, MCI operator 05 06 19 19.

Sleeping in Paris (about 6F = US$1)

Paris is a huge city with a huge selection of hotels. To keep things manageable, I've focused on three safe, handy, and colorful neighborhoods, listing good hotels

in each neighborhood to help make you a temporary resi-
dent. Good restaurants and cafés for each area are listed
below, under Restaurants.

Choose your price range and your neighborhood. A
hotel's star classification is indicated by an *. Old, characteristic, budget Parisian hotels have always been cramped.
Now they've added elevators, W.C.'s, and private showers,
and are even more cramped.

While you can save up to 100F by finding the increas-
ingly rare room without a shower, these rooms are often
smaller, and many places charge around 20F for each
shower you take down the hall. Remember, baths and
twin beds cost more than showers and double beds. And
a toilet in the room costs even more. Breakfasts are usually
optional and 20 to 30F (prices listed are without breakfast). You can save about 10F each by eating in a nearby
café. Singles, unless the hotel has a few closet-type rooms
that fit only one twin bed, are simply doubles inhabited
by one person, only about 20 to 50F less than a double.

Assume Paris will be tight. Look early or have a reservation. Conventions clog the city in September (worst),
October, May, and June. July and August are easier. Most
hotels accept telephone reservations only for today or
tomorrow until about midday. Most will have and hold a
room for you if you call just after breakfast. Most require
prepayment for a reservation far in advance (call first, and
if they won't take a credit card number, follow up with a
$50 traveler's check or a bank check in francs for the first
night). Some, usually the very cheapest places, take no
reservations at all.

**Hotels in the Rue Cler Neighborhood—7th dis-
trict, Métro: École Militaire, postal code 75007:** Rue
Cler, a village-like pedestrian street, is safe, tidy, and
makes me feel like I must have been a poodle in a pre-
vious life. How such coziness lodged itself between the
high-powered government-business district and the
expensive Eiffel Tower and Invalides areas, I'll never
know. This is the ideal place to call home in Paris. Living
here ranks with the top museums as one of the city's
great experiences.

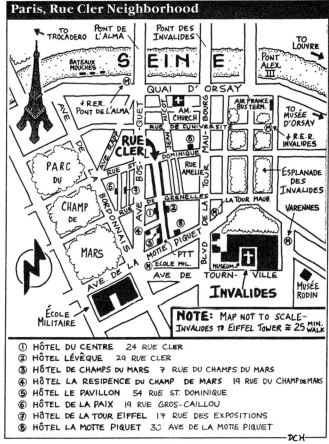

Paris, Rue Cler Neighborhood

① HÔTEL DU CENTRE   24 RUE CLER
② HÔTEL LÉVÊQUE   29 RUE CLER
③ HÔTEL DE CHAMPS DU MARS   7 RUE DU CHAMPS DU MARS
④ HÔTEL LA RESIDENCE DU CHAMP DE MARS   19 RUE DU CHAMP DE MARS
⑤ HÔTEL LE PAVILLON   54 RUE ST. DOMINIQUE
⑥ HÔTEL DE LA PAIX   19 RUE GROS-CAILLOU
⑦ HÔTEL DE LA TOUR EIFFEL   17 RUE DES EXPOSITIONS
⑧ HÔTEL LA MOTTE PIQUET   30 AVE DE LA MOTTE PIQUET

On rue Cler, you can step outside your hotel and eat and browse your way through a street full of tart shops, colorful outdoor produce stalls, cheeseries, and fish vendors. And you're within an easy walk of the Eiffel Tower, Les Invalides, and the Seine, as well as the Orsay and Rodin museums.

Hôtel Leveque (* 190-300F, 29 rue Cler, tel. 47 05 49 15, fax 45 50 49 36 for reservation confirmations, English normally spoken, except by friendly Michele, who is very creative at communicating) is simple, clean, and well run, with a helpful staff, a singing maid, and, thanks to a warm spot in owner Françoise's heart, the cheapest breakfast

(20F) on the block. Reserve by phone; leave Visa number. No elevator, right in the traffic-free rue Cler thick of things.

The **Hôtel du Centre** (* 300F doubles, all with TV and shower, five cheap 170F doubles, 28F breakfast, 24 rue Cler, tel. 47 05 52 33), across the street from Leveque, has a few Eiffel Tower view rooms, is funkier, frumpier, and a bit less free flowing than the Leveque. The Greze family accepts telephone reservations with a credit card.

The **Hôtel du Champs de Mars** (** 310-340F doubles, all with shower or bath, 30F breakfast, 7 rue du Champs de Mars, tel. 45 51 52 30), with its fine rooms and a helpful English-speaking staff, is a top "normal hotel" rue Cler option.

Hôtel la Motte Piquet (** 310-400F doubles, 30 ave. de la Motte Piquet, on the corner of rue Cler, tel. 47 05 09 57), with a plush lobby and basic comfortable rooms, is high on gadgets and low on charm.

Hôtel Muguet (** 230-340F doubles, 30F breakfast, 11 rue Chevert, tel. 47 05 05 93, fax 45 50 25 37) is a great value on a quiet bland street two blocks toward Les Invalides from rue Cler. Most of its rooms are big, many with extra sitting rooms. The upper floors offer balconettes with Eiffel views. It's a plain, antique-lampshades, kittens-and-flowers kind of place, very French, with worn carpets, sloping floors, an elevator, and homey public rooms.

Hôtel de la Paix (* 235F doubles all with shower, 385F triples, and four 130F singles without showers, 26F breakfast, 19 rue Gros-Caillou, tel. 45 51 86 17) is a well-worn, spartan place, run very aggreeably by English-speaking Noël. If you want cheap twin beds, bright bed lights, and easy telephone reservations, this is a gem. No elevator, peeling plaster.

Hôtel de la Tour Eiffel (** 380-450F doubles, 25F breakfast, 17 rue des Expositions, tel. 47 05 14 75), with petite but wicker-pleasant rooms, all with private facilities and TVs, is like a small salad with too much dressing.

Hôtel Eiffel Rive Gauche (** 340-400F doubles, all with showers, TV, and phone, 6 rue de Gros Caillou, tel.

45 51 24 56, secure phone reservation with Visa number) is a decent value on a quiet street, with a tiny leafy court-yard giving the place a little more brightness than average.

Hôtel Malar Paris (* 260F doubles all with bath or shower, has a good 4-bed family room, 29 rue Malar, tel. 45 51 38 46) is cozy, quiet, and very French.

Résidence Latour Maubourg (** 400-500F doubles with a few simple 210F doubles, 150 rue de Grenelle, tel. 45 51 75 28) is an Old World splurge with spacious rooms.

Rue Cler Helpful Hints: Become a local at a rue Cler café for breakfast, or join the afternoon crowd for *une bière pression* (a draft beer). Cute shops and bakeries line rue Cler, and there's a self-serve laundry at 16 rue Cler and another (more expensive) just off rue Cler on rue de la Grenelle. The métro station and a post office with phone booths are at the end of rue Cler, on avenue de la Motte Piquet. Your neighborhood TI is at the Tour Eiffel (open May-September 11:00-18:00, tel. 45 51 22 15).

At 65 quai d'Orsay, you'll find the **American Church and College**, the community center for Americans living in Paris. The interdenominational service at 11:00 on Sundays and coffee-fellowship and 50F lunch feast that follow are a great way to make some friends and get a taste of émigré life in Paris. Stop by and pick up copies of the *Free Voice* and *France-U.S.A. Contacts* newspapers (tel. 47 05 07 99). There's a handy bulletin board for those in need of housing or work through the community of 30,000 Americans living in Paris.

Afternoon *boules* (lawn bowling) on the esplanade des Invalides is competitive and a relaxing spectator sport. Look for the dirt area to the upper right as you face the Invalides.

For a magical picnic dinner, assemble it in no less than six stops on rue Cler and lounge on the best grass in Paris (the police don't mind after dark) with the dogs, frisbees, a floodlit Eiffel Tower, and a cool breeze in the Parc du Champs de Mars. For an after-dinner cruise, it's just a short walk across the river (Pont d'Alma) to the Bâteaux Mouches.

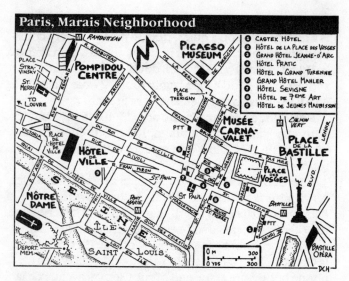

Paris, Marais Neighborhood

1 Castex Hôtel
2 Hôtel de la Place des Vosges
3 Grand Hôtel Jeanne-d'Arc
4 Hôtel Pratic
5 Hôtel du Grand Turenne
6 Grand Hôtel Mahler
7 Hôtel Sevigne
8 Hôtel de 7ème Art
9 Hôtel de Jeunes Maubisson

Hotels in the Marais—4th district, Métro: St. Paul, postal code 75004: Those interested in a more Soho/ Greenwich, gentrified, urban jungle locale would enjoy making the Marais-Jewish Quarter-St. Paul-Vosges area their Parisian home. The Marais is a cheaper and definitely a more happening locale than rue Cler. Narrow medieval Paris at its finest, only fifteen years ago it was a forgotten Parisian backwater. The Marais is now one of Paris's most popular residential areas. It's a very short walk to Notre-Dame, Île St. Louis, and the Latin Quarter. The Métro stop St. Paul puts you right in the heart of the Marais.

Castex Hôtel (* 240-280F doubles, all with showers, 25F breakfast, 5 rue Castex, just off place de la Bastille and rue Saint Antoine, Métro: Bastille, tel. 42 72 31 52, fax 42 72 57 91) is newly renovated, clean, cheery, quiet, and run by the very friendly Bouchand family (son Blaise, pronounced blaze, speaks English). This place is a great value, with the distinctly un-Parisian characteristic of seeming like it wants your business. Reserve by phone and leave your Visa number.

Hôtel de la Place des Vosges (** 370F doubles all with shower, 33F breakfast, 12 rue de Biraque, just off the elegant place des Vosges, tel. 42 72 60 46, fax 42 72 02 64,

English spoken, Visa accepted) is classy with a freshly made, antique feel, friendly, and well run, with 14 rooms on a quiet street.

Grand Hôtel Jeanne d'Arc (** 360F doubles, 410F triples, 460F quads, 27F breakfast, 3 rue Jarente, 75004 Paris, tel. 48 87 62 11), a plush place on a quiet street just off a cozy square, is the best normal hotel option in the Marais. Its 38 rooms all have shower or bath, TV, telephone, and W.C. Like the rest of the hotel, the breakfast room is elegant.

Hôtel Pratic (* 180-280F doubles, 9 rue d'Ormesson, 75004 Paris, tel. 48 87 80 47) has a slightly Arabic feel in its cramped lobby. The rooms are fine, and it's right on a great, people-friendly square.

Hôtel du Grand Turenne (** 450F doubles, 6 rue de Turenne, tel. 42 78 43 25, fax 42 78 50 66, English spoken) is being renovated but promises not to destroy its classy old atmosphere. All the comforts and an excellent location.

Grand Hôtel Mahler (* 160-280F doubles, 5 rue Mahler, tel. 42 72 60 92, fax 42 72 25 37) should be "grand old" Hôtel Mahler. This very French place makes me nostalgic for all my old favorites that got renovated. No elevator, so many coats of paint that the molding is fading, and run by people who believe French is the only worthwhile language.

Hôtel Sevigne (* 250-290F, required 16F breakfast, 2 rue Mahler, tel. 42 72 76 17) is likable only for its practicality, location, and price.

Hôtel de 7ème Art (** 360F doubles, all with shower, W.C., and TV, 20 rue St. Paul, tel. 42 77 04 03, fax 42 77 69 10) is a Hollywood nostalgia place run by young hip Marais types with a full service café/bar and Charlie Chaplin murals.

Hôtel de Jeunes Maubisson (70F beds in 4-bed rooms, noon to 16:00 lockout, 10 rue des Barres, Métro: Pont-Marie, tel. 42 72 72 09) is Paris's most elegant *foyer* (hostel), designed for travelers 18-35 years old and groups. Its location is great and the atmosphere comfortable.

Marais Helpful Hints: Place des Vosges is Paris's oldest square, built for Henry IV. Victor Hugo lived at #6 (small museum). The nearby Musée Carnavalet offers your best look at the last 500 years of Parisian history. Rue des Rosiers is main-street Paris for the Orthodox Jewish community. The new opera house is just to the east, and a short wander to the west takes you into the hopping Beaubourg/Les Halles area. Paris's biggest and best budget department store is BHV, next to the Hôtel de Ville. Marais post offices are across from Hôtel Castex on rue Castex and on the corner of rue Pavée and Franc Bourgois.

Hotels in the Contrescarpe Neighborhood—5th district, Métro: Monge, postal code 75005: This neighborhood is over the hill from the Latin Quarter, five minutes from the Panthéon and an easy walk to Notre-Dame, Île de la Cité, Île St. Louis, and blvds. St. Germain and St. Michel. Stay here if you like to be close to the action, which in the summer will be mostly tourist action. The rue Mouffetard and place Contrescarpe are the thriving heart and soul of the neighborhood, a market street by day and restaurant row by night. Listed here are one elegant, hard-to-get-into gem and three rock-bottom dives.

The **Hôtel des Grandes Écoles** (** 300-500F doubles, 30F breakfast, 75 rue de Cardinal Lemoine, tel. 43 26 79 23, fax 43 25 28 15) is a friendly and peaceful oasis with three buildings protecting its own garden courtyard. This place is very popular, so call far in advance or try your luck in the morning. Their cheapest rooms are nearly bad but their top rooms are elegant.

Hôtel Central (* 200F doubles, all with showers, 6 rue Descartes, tel. 46 33 57 93) has a romantic location, a steep and slippery, castlelike stairway, and stark rooms with saggy beds and meek showers. Nothing fancy, but very Parisian.

The low-key and bare bones **Hôtel du Commerce** (no stars, 110-140F doubles, no breakfast, 14 rue de La Montagne Sainte-Geneviève, Métro: Place Maubert, tel. 43 54 89 69, takes no reservations, call at 10:00 and he'll say *"oui"* or *"non"*) is run by Monsieur Mattuzzi, who must be a pirate gone good. He brags that the place is 300 years old. Judging by the vinyl in the halls, I believe him. It's a great rock-bottom deal and as safe as any dive next to the police station can be. In the morning, the landlady will knock and chirp *"Restez-vous?"* ("Are you staying for one more night?").

Y&H (young and happy) Hostel: Great location, easygoing, hip management, but depressing showers and generally crowded and filthy conditions. Four- to eight-bed rooms. Closed from 11:00 to 17:00, no reservations but call to see what's open (80F per bed plus 10F for sheets, 80 rue Mouffetard, tel. 45 35 09 53).

Contrescarpe Helpful Hints: The Contrescarpe neighborhood's PTT is between rue Mouffetard and rue Monge at 10 rue de l'Épée du Bois. Place Monge hosts a colorful outdoor market on Wednesdays, Fridays, and Sundays until 13:00. The street market at the bottom of rue Mouffetard bustles daily, 8:00-12:00 and 15:30-19:00.

The Jardin des Plantes is close by and great for evening walks. But those in the know will head through the doorway at 49 rue Monge and into the surprising Roman Arena de Lutèce. Today, boules players occupy the stage while couples cuddle on the stone bleachers. Walk over to the Panthéon, admire it from the outside, but go into the wildly beautiful St. Étienne-du-Mont church.

Eating in Paris
Everything goes here. Paris is France's wine and cuisine melting pot. While it lacks a distinctive style of its own, it draws from the best of all French provinces.

Paris could hold a gourmet's Olympics—and import nothing. Picnic or go to snack bars for quick lunches and linger longer over dinner. You can eat very well, restaurant-style, for 120F. Ask your hotel to recommend a small restaurant nearby in the 80 to 100 franc range. Famous places are often overpriced, overcrowded, and overrated. Find a quiet neighborhood and wander, or follow a local recommendation.

Cafeterias and Picnics

Many Parisian department stores have top floor cafeterias offering not really cheap, but low-risk, low-stress, what-you-see-is-what-you-get, quick budget meals. Try **Samaritaine** (Pont-Neuf near the Louvre, 5th floor) or **Mélodine** (Métro: Rambuteau, next to the Pompidou Center, open daily 11:00-22:00). The French word for self-service is *self-service*.

For picnics, you'll find handy little groceries all over town (but rarely near famous sights). Good picnic fixings include roasted chicken, half-liter boxes of demi-crème (2%) milk, drinkable yogurt, fresh bakery goods, melons, and exotic pâtés and cheeses. Great take-out deli-type foods like gourmet salads and quiches abound. While in the United States wine is taboo in public places, this is *pas de problème* in France. Most shops close from around 12:30 to 14:00.

The ultimate classy picnic shopping place is **Fauchon**—the famous "best gourmet grocery in France." It's fast and expensive but cheaper than a restaurant (26 place de la Madeleine, behind the Madeleine Church, Métro: Madeleine, open 9:30-19:00, closed Sunday). There's a stand-up bar in the bakery across the street. If you're hungry near Notre-Dame, the only grocery store on the Île de la Cité is tucked away on a small street running parallel to the church, one block north.

Good Picnic Spots: The pedestrian bridge, Pont des Arts, with unmatched views and plentiful benches, is great. Bring your own dinner feast and watch the riverboats light up the city for you. The Palais Royal across the street from the Louvre is a good spot for a peaceful and royal lunchtime picnic. Or try the little triangular Henry IV Park on the west tip of the Île de la Cité, people-watching at the Pompidou Center or in the elegant place des Vosges, at the Rodin Museum, or after dark in the Eiffel Tower park (Champs de Mars).

Restaurants (by neighborhood)

Of course the Parisian eating scene is kept at a rolling boil, and entire books are written and lives are spent on the subject. Here are a few places to consider, listed by neighborhood, to work smoothly into your busy sight-seeing strategy. If you'd like to visit a district specifically to eat, consider the colorful, touristic but fun string of eateries along rue Mouffetard behind the Panthéon; Montmartre, which is very touristy around the place du Tetre but hides some vampy values in the side streets; and the well-worn Latin Quarter (see below).

Rue Cler and Invalides: The rue Cler neighborhood isn't famous for its restaurants. That's why I eat here. **Restaurant La Serre** (51 rue Cler) is friendly and reasonable. **Le Petit Niçois**, across from Hôtel Amelie at rue Amelie, with the best moderately priced seafood in the area, is where locals go for bouillabaise (fish stew). **Au Café de Mars**, on the corner of rue Augerau and Gros Caillou, is a contemporary Parisian café/restaurant with sumptuous cuisine, fair prices, and an English-speaking staff. **Le Petit Bosquet** (29 rue de l'Exposition) is friendly and popular, serving Hungarian cuisine in simple surroundings at reasonable prices. **L'Ami de Jean** (near Hôtel Malar at 29 rue Malar) is a lively place to sample Basque cuisine. Bring your own beret and rosy cheeks. The **Ambassade du Sud-Ouest** is a locally popular wine store cum restaurant specializing in southwestern cuisine. Try the *daubes de canard* and toast your own bread (46 ave. de la Bourdonnais, tel. 45 55 59 59). The best and most traditional French brasserie in the area is the dressy **Thoumieux** (79 rue St. Dominique, tel. 47 05 49 75). For a good intimate restaurant with a friendly, English-speaking manager and a 100F menu eat at **Restaurant Le Verdois** (19:30-22:15 for dinner, closed Sunday, 19 ave. de la Motte Piquet, just off rue Cler, tel. 45 55 40 38). For a quick sit-down or take-out meal, **Tarte Julie's** is just right (28 rue Cler).

The Marais: The candlelit windows of the Marais are filled with munching sophisticates. The epicenter of all this charm is the tiny square where rue Caron and rue d'Ormesson intersect, midway between the St. Paul métro stop and the place des Vosges. For more conspicuous elegance a coffee or light lunch on the place des

Vosges is good. Hobos with taste picnic on the place des
Vosges itself, trying not to make the local mothers with
children nervous (closed at night). For a memorable picnic dinner, ten minutes from the Marais, cross the river to
Île St. Louis and find a river-level bench on the tip facing
Île de la Cité. **Mexico Magico** (Rue du Vielle du Temple
and Rue des Coutures St. Gervais) is small, fun mariachi à
la française. . . Paris's best Mexican restaurant. **Rélais de
St. Paul** (31 rue François Miron) is cozy and classy, with a
110F four-course menu. **L'Énoteca** (across from Hôtel du
7ème Art at 20 rue St. Paul) has cheap, lively Italian cuisine in a relaxed, open setting. **Auberge de Jarente** (7
rue Jarente) is another popular, atmospheric, and reasonable eatery.

    Latin Quarter: La Petite Bouclerie is a cozy place
with classy family cooking (moderate, 33 rue de la Harpe,
center of touristy Latin Quarter). Friendly Monsieur
Millon runs **Restaurant Polidor**, an old turn-of-the-
century-style place, with great *cuisine bourgeois*, a
vigorous local crowd, and a historic toilet. Arrive at 19:00
to get a seat. . . in the restaurant, that is (moderate, 41 rue
Monsieur le Prince, midway between Odéon and Luxembourg métro stops, tel. 43 26 95 34). **Atelier Maître
Albert** fills with Left Bank types. The best value is its
nightly fixed-price meal (dinner only, closed Sunday, 5 rue
Maître Albert, Métro: Maubert Mutualité, tel. 46 33 13 78).

    Île St. Louis: Cruise the island's main street for a vari-
ety of good options. For crazy (but touristy and expensive) cellar atmosphere and hearty fun food, feast at **La
Taverne du Sergent Recruiter.** The "Sergeant
Recruiter" used to get young Parisians drunk and stuffed
here, then sign them into the army. It's all-you-can-eat,
including wine and service, for 180F (41 rue St. Louis, in
the center of Île St. Louis, 3 minutes from Notre-Dame,
open Monday-Saturday from 19:00, tel. 43 54 75 42).
There's a just-this-side-of-a-food-fight clone next door
at **Nos Ancêtres Les Gaulois** (Our Ancestors the Gauls,
39 rue St. Louis-en-l'Île, tel. 46 33 66 07, open daily at
19:00).

Pompidou Center: The popular and very French **Café de la Cité** has long wooden tables and great lunch specials (inexpensive, 22 rue Rambuteau, Métro: Rambuteau, open daily except Sunday). The **Mélodine** self-service is right at the Rambuteau métro stop.

For an elegant splurge surrounded by lavish art nouveau decor, dine at **Julien** (250F meals with wine, 16 rue du Faubourg St. Denis, Métro: Strasbourg-St. Denis, tel. 47 70 12 06, make reservations).

Near Place de la Concorde: André Fauré serves basic, hearty, all-you-can-eat-and-drink, French farm-style meals for a very good price (40 rue du Mont Thabor, Métro: Concorde Madeleine, tel. 42 60 74 28, open Monday-Saturday 12:00-15:00, 19:00-22:30).

Near the Louvre: L'Incroyable serves *incroyable* meals at an equally *incroyable* price—cheap (26 rue de Richelieu, Métro: Palais-Royal, in a narrow passage between 23 rue de Montpensier and 26 rue de Richelieu, open Tuesday-Saturday 11:45-14:30, 18:30-20:30).

Near Arc de Triomphe: L'Étoile Verte (The Green Star) is a great working-class favorite (inexpensive, 13 rue Brey, between Wagram and MacMahon, Métro: Étoile).

Three gourmet working-class fixtures in Paris are: **Le Chartier** (7 rue du Faubourge Montmartre, Métro: Montmartre), **Le Commerce** (51 rue du Commerce, Métro: Commerce) and **Le Drouot** (103 rue de Richelieu, Métro: Richelieu-Drouot). Each wraps very cheap and basic food in a bustling, unpretentious atmosphere.

First Evening Orientation Walk (ideal for jet laggards)

Once you've set up in your hotel, introduce yourself to Paris. If you just landed in Europe, an evening walk will show you some of Paris's delights and keep your jet laggy body moving until a reasonable European bedtime. Whenever you run out of steam, just find the nearest Métro and head back home.

Start with a Métro ride to the Louvre stop (Métro: Louvre). Study the Métro lesson above and use this ride

LOUVRE Metro

to put each of those tips into action. Exit the station, walk
to the river, jog right, and cross the pedestrian-only
bridge (Pont des Arts). The view up and down the river is
breathtaking. Take your time and lots of photos here, and
grab a bench. On the Left Bank, find your way around
the right side of the Palais de l'Institut de France, part of
which is Académie Français, to the rue de Seine. Consider
a stop at the very Parisian La Palette café, then take a brief
right on rue de Buci. Take a left onto the famous boulevard St. Germain, the heart and soul of Paris cafés and
shopping. Look for Paris's most expensive café, Au Deux
Magots, as soon as you enter St. Germain. (Hemingway
hung out here while writing *The Sun Also Rises*, back
when they didn't charge $8 for a glass of champagne.)
Check out the recently restored St. Germain des Pres
Church, then cruise the boulevard St. Germain, making a
right at the place de l'Odéon. Meander around the
temple-like Theatre de l'Odéon into Paris's most beautiful park, the Luxembourg Gardens. Grab a chair by the
center fountain and contemplate where you are—as
Hemingway loved to do, right here. (The handiest Métro
stop from here is Luxembourg or Odéon, back on boulevard St. Germain.)

PARIS IN THREE DAYS

Our busy plan of attack is outlined here, with walking guides for each day. Refer to the sight descriptions as you plan your days and do these walks.

Suggested Schedule Day 2

7:30	Breakfast.
8:30	Start at place St. Michel (Métro: St. Michel), walk through Latin Quarter to Notre-Dame.
9:00	Tour Notre-Dame.
10:00	Deportation Memorial.
10:30	Tour Ste. Chapelle.
11:30	Lunch at Samaritaine.
13:00	Tour the Louvre, hopefully with a guide.
15:00	Stroll the Tuileries. Stop for a drink at one of the garden cafés, then metro from the "Concorde" stop to "Étoile" to see the Arc de Triomphe. If you have time and energy, walk down the Champs-Élysées.
19:30	Dinner, possibly followed by a Seine cruise.

Suggested Schedule Day 3

8:00	Breakfast.
8:30	Métro to Trocadero, follow fountains to Eiffel Tower.
9:30	Ride the elevator to the second level—what a view!
10:30	Walk through Champs de Mars to rue Cler. Pick up picnic goodies here and maybe stop for a café break.
11:15	Skirt the Hôtel des Invalides; admire it from outside.
11:30	Rodin Museum tour and backyard picnic.
13:30	Tour Musée d'Orsay.
16:00	Stroll along boulevard St. Germain into Latin Quarter.
19:00	Head up to Montmartre and mainline the romance of Paris.

Suggested Schedule Day 4

8:30	Breakfast.
9:00	Métro to Hôtel de Ville.
9:45	Walking tour of Île St. Louis.
10:30	On to Le Marais and place des Vosges.
11:30	Tour Picasso Museum or Carnavalet Museum.
13:00	Fast lunch on rue Rosiers, the heart of Jewish Paris.
13:45	Mosey on to the Pompidou Center, walk Rambuteau to Les Halles, and catch the Métro/RER to Versailles. (Or, see the Museum of Modern Art and enjoy the area.)
15:30	Arrive in Versailles, tour palace, Little Hamlet. Dinner back in Paris.

Day 2 Paris Walk

Last night we oriented; today we attack. Start at the St. Michel Métro stop, where you'll find the heart of an uncharacteristically sleepy Latin Quarter. This is a street-hoppin' place at night. It uses mornings to recover. Walk down rue de la Huchette (past the popular jazz cellar at #5—check the schedule) and over the bridge to Notre-Dame Cathedral. It took 200 years to build this church. Walk around to its impressive back side and visit the moving memorial to the 200,000 French people deported by Hitler in World War II. Across the bridge is the Île, or island, of St. Louis (we'll tour it later). Walking back through the center of the Île de la Cité, you'll come to the Ste. Chapelle church, a newly restored Gothic gem. After touring it, continue to the tip of the island (lovely park) through the peaceful, triangular place Dauphine. Next, cross the oldest bridge in town, the Pont Neuf, to the Right Bank. Drop into the Samaritaine department store across the bridge—don't miss the remarkable interior of this French "J. C. Penneys." Lunch on the fifth floor (cafeteria open 11:30-15:00, 15:30-18:30). Then tackle the Louvre, at one time Europe's grandest palace and today its most grueling and overwhelming museum. The new Louvre entry is a magnificent glass pyramid in the central courtyard. After mastering the Louvre, unwind with a

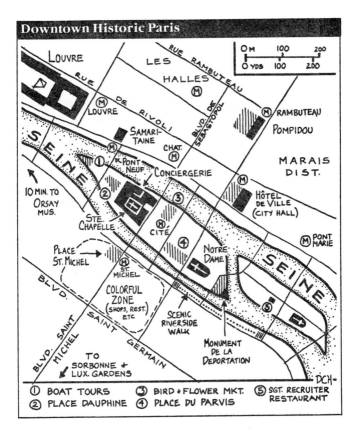

Downtown Historic Paris

① BOAT TOURS   ③ BIRD + FLOWER MKT.   ⑤ SGT. RECRUITER RESTAURANT
② PLACE DAUPHINE   ④ PLACE DU PARVIS

stroll through the Tuileries to the place de la Concorde, where over 1,300 heads rolled during the French Revolution, and bop up the world's most famous street, the Champs-Élysées. From the majestic Arc de Triomphe, you can take the métro home.

Day 3 Paris Walk

Métro to Trocadéro. Exit the subway, following the Sortie Tour Eiffel signs to one of Europe's great views. From here, the tower seems to straddle the military school (École Militaire). Napoleon lies powerfully dead under the dome of Les Invalides to the left. Take the elevator up to the second level of the tower, then walk away from the river through the park. Follow the third cross street left

into the classy area around rue de Grenelle. Turn right on
rue Cler for a rare bit of village Paris (shops closed
13:00-16:00 and on Monday). Assemble a picnic and follow avenue de la Motte Piquet left to the grand esplanade
des Invalides. The Hôtel des Invalides, with Napoleon's
tomb and the army museum, is on your right. Cross the
square, turn right on avenue des Invalides and look for
the Rodin Museum (Hôtel Biron) on the left. Tour the
great sculpture museum. Picnic or eat in the cafeteria surrounded by Rodin's works in the elegant backyard.

Now it's on to the dazzling Musée d'Orsay. Make a right
when you come out of the Rodin Museum and a quick
left on rue de Bourgogne; follow it to the Assemblée
Nationale, where you'll turn right on rue de l'Université,
cross boulevard St. Germain, and follow signs to the
Musée d'Orsay. If you still have energy after this museum,
walk away from the river and hook up with Paris's best
people-watching, shopping, and café street, the boulevard St. Germain.

Day 4 Paris Walk
Start in front of the Hôtel de Ville, the old city hall (Métro:
Hôtel de Ville). Admire the superb restoration, then follow the river down to the Pont Louis Phillipe. Cross it
into the charm and tranquillity of the Île St. Louis. Bisect
the island along rue St. Louis (good place for dinner
tonight), admiring the doorway at #51 and the minuscule
travel bookstore at #35, then take the last left across the
Pont de Sully and angle up the rue du Petit Musc. Make
your way into the most beautiful square in Paris, the place
des Vosges. Now it's decision time: are you a Picasso fan
or more curious about Parisian history? Tour either the
Picasso Museum or the Carnavalet Museum, then drop
down to the rue Rosiers for some character and lunch or
grab a falafel sandwich to go. Resume your stroll down
rue Rosiers and turn right when it ends. A left on rue des
Francs Bourgeois brings you back to the twentieth century with the bizarre architecture of the Pompidou Center. Join the fray around the center and take in a street
show or two. Ride the escalators through the Star Wars

tubes of the Pompidou to the top for the view and consider seeing its excellent modern art collection on the
fourth floor. (See Beaubourg Sightseeing Highlights for
more information and ideas on the Beaubourg area.)

Sightseeing Highlights
Reminder: Nearly all Parisian museums are closed on
Tuesday. Those that aren't (e.g., Orsay, Rodin) normally
close on Monday. Most have shorter hours on Sunday and
from October through March. And many start closing
down rooms 30 minutes before the actual closing time.
Museum holidays are usually 1/1, 5/1, 5/8, 7/14, 11/1,
11/11, and 12/25. Those under 26 and over 60 get big discounts on most sights.
▲▲**Latin Quarter**—This area, which gets its name from
the language used here when it was an exclusive medieval
university district, lies between the Luxembourg Gardens
and the Seine, centering around the Sorbonne University
and boulevards St. Germain and St. Michel. This is the
core of the Left Bank—the artsy, liberal, hippy, Bohemian
district of poets, philosophers, and winos. It's full of
international eateries, far-out bookshops, street singers,
pale girls in black berets, and jazz clubs. For colorful wan-
dering and café-sitting, afternoons and evenings are best.
▲▲**Notre-Dame Cathedral**—The cathedral is 700
years old and packed with history and tourists. Climb to
the top (entrance on outside left, open 9:00-17:00, you
get over 400 stairs for only 30F) for a great gargoyle's-eye
view of the city. Study its sculpture (Notre-Dame's forte)
and windows, take in a mass (or the free Sunday 17:15
recital on the 6,000-pipe organ, France's largest), eaves-
drop on guides, walk all around the outside. (Open
8:00-19:00, treasury open 9:30-18:00, admission free.
Ask about the free English tours, normally Tuesdays and
Wednesdays in July and August at noon. Tel. 43 26 07 39.
Clean 2.50F toilets are in front of the church near Charlemagne's statue.)
    Back outside, the archaeological crypt offers a fascinat-
ing look at the remains of the earlier city and church
(enter 100 yards in front of church, daily 10:00-17:30).

Drop into Hôtel Dieu, on the square opposite the river,
for a pleasant courtyard and a look at a modern hospice,
offering many a pleasant last stop before heaven.

▲▲**Deportation Memorial**—The architecture of this
memorial to the French victims of the Nazi concentration
camps is a powerful blend of water, sky, bars, confine-
ment, concrete, eternal flame, the names of many concentration camps, and a crystal for each of the 200,000
victims. (Open at 10:00, east tip of the island near Île St.
Louis, behind Notre-Dame, free.)

▲▲▲**Sainte-Chapelle**—The triumph of Gothic church
architecture, a cathedral of glass, like none other. It was
built in just five years to house the supposed Crown of
Thorns (which cost the king more than the church).
Downstairs was for commoners, upstairs for royal Chris-
tians. Hang out at the top of the spiral stairs and watch the
room's beauty suck the breath from emerging tourists.
There's a good little book with color photos on sale that
explains the stained glass in English. There are concerts
almost every summer evening (120F). Anything going on
tonight? Even a beginning violin class would sound
lovely here. (Open 9:30-18:00, 24F. Stop at the ticket
booth outside the church, or call 43 54 30 09 for concert
information. Handy free public toilets just outside.)

▲▲▲**The Louvre**—This is Europe's oldest, biggest,
greatest, and maybe most crowded museum. Don't try to
cover it thoroughly. The 90-minute English language tour
is the best way to enjoy this huge museum (find Accueil
des Groupes desk at entry, information tel. 40 20 50 50,
normally nearly hourly, 24F). *Mona Winks* (buy in U.S.A.)
includes a self-guided tour of the Louvre as well as of the
Orsay, the Pompidou, and Versailles.

If you're unable to get a guide, a good do-it-yourself
tour of the museum's highlights would include (in this
order, starting in the Denon wing) Ancient Greek (Parthe-
non frieze, Venus de Milo, Nike of Samothrace); Apollo
Gallery (jewels); French and Italian paintings in the
Grande Galerie (a quarter-mile long and worth the hike);
the Mona Lisa and her Italian Renaissance roommates; the
nearby neoclassical collection (*Coronation of Napoleon*);

and the romantic collection with works by Delacroix and
Gericault. (Open 9:00-18:00, Wednesday until 21:30,
most of the collection on Monday until 21:30. Closed
Tuesday. 30F, 15F for the young, the old, and those who
visit on Sunday. Tel. 40 20 53 17 or 40 20 51 51 for
recorded information. Métro: Palais-Royale/Musée du
Louvre.)

▲▲▲ **Orsay Museum**—This is Paris's long-awaited
nineteenth-century art museum (actually, art from
1848-1914), including Europe's greatest collection of
Impressionist works (call for 25F English tour schedule).

Start on the ground floor. The conservative establish-
ment "pretty" art is on the right, then cross left into the
brutally truthful and, at the time, very shocking art of the
realist rebels and Manet. Then go way up the escalator at
the far end to the series of impressionist rooms (Monet,
Renoir, Degas, et al.) and van Gogh. Don't miss the art
nouveau on the mezzanine level. The museum is housed
in a former train station (Gare d'Orsay) across the river
and 10 minutes downstream from the Louvre. (Open
9:00-17:30 in July and August and all Sundays, 10:00-17:30
other days, Thursday until 21:45, closed Monday, most
crowded around 11:00 and 14:00. 30F, 15F for the young
and the old, tel. 40 49 48 84.)

▲▲ **Napoleon's Tomb and the Army Museum**—The
emperor lies majestically dead under a grand dome—a
goose-bumping pilgrimage for historians—surrounded
by the tombs of other French war heroes and Europe's
greatest military museum, in the Hôtel des Invalides.
(Open daily 10:00-18:00, 25F, tel. 45 55 37 70. Métro: La
Tour Maubourg.)

▲▲ **Rodin Museum**—This user-friendly museum is
filled with surprisingly entertaining work by the greatest
sculptor since Michelangelo. See *The Kiss, The Thinker,*
and many more. Near Napoleon's Tomb. (Open 10:00-18:00,
closed Monday; 20F, half-price on Sunday, tel. 47 05 01
34. Métro: Varennes, 75007. Cafeteria and great picnic
spots in back garden.)

▲ **Pompidou Center**—Europe's greatest collection of
far-out modern art, the Musée National d'Art Moderne is

housed in this colorfully exoskeletal building. After so
many Madonnas and Children, a piano smashed to bits
and glued to the wall is refreshing. It's a social center with
lots of people, street theater, and activity inside and
out—a perpetual street fair. Ride the escalator for a free
city view from the café terrace on top. (Open Monday-
Friday 12:00-22:00, Saturday, Sunday, and most holidays
10:00-22:00, closed Tuesday; 27F, free Sunday from
10:00-14:00; tel. 42 77 12 33, Métro: Rambuteau.)

▲**Beaubourg**—This was a separate village until the
twelfth century, and today it includes the area from the
Pompidou Center to the Forum des Halles shopping center. Most of Paris's hip renovation energy over the past 20
years seems to have been directed here—before then it
was a slum. Don't miss the new wave fountains (the *Hom-
age to Stravinsky*) on the river side of the Pompidou
Center or the eerie clock you'll find through the *Quartier
d'Horloge* passage on the other side of the Pompidou
Center. A colorful stroll down rue Rambuteau takes you to
the space age Forum des Halles shopping center, on the
site of what was a wonderful outdoor food market. As
you tour this shopping mecca, peek into the huge 350-
year-old St. Eustache Church and admire the unusual
glass chandeliered altar. The striking round building at
the end of the esplanade is Paris's old Bourse, or Commercial Exchange. For an oasis of peace, continue on to
the interior gardens of the Palais-Royal. (Métro: Les Halles
or Rambuteau.)

▲▲**Eiffel Tower**—Crowded and expensive but worth
the trouble. The higher you go, the more you pay. I think
the view from the 400-foot-high second level is plenty.
Pilier Nord (the north pillar) has the biggest elevator—
with the fastest moving line. The Restaurant Belle France
serves decent 70F meals (first level). Don't miss the entertaining free movie on the history of the tower on the first
level. Heck of a view. (Open daily 9:00-23:00; 18F to the
first level, 34F to the second, 50F to go all the way for the
1,000-foot view. On a budget? You can climb the stairs to
the second level for only 9F. Arrive early for less crowds.
Tel. 45 50 34 56. Métro: Trocadero. RER: Champs de

Mars.) For another great view, especially at night, cross
the river and enjoy the tower from Trocadero.

▲**Montparnasse Tower**—A 59-floor superscraper,
cheaper and easier to get to the top than the Eiffel Tower.
Possibly Paris's best view since the Eiffel Tower is in it.
Buy the photo-guide to the city, go to the rooftop and
orient yourself. This is a fine way to understand the lay of
this magnificent land. It's a good place to be as the sun
goes down on your first day in Paris. Find your hotel,
retrace your day's steps, locate the famous buildings.
(Open summer 9:30-23:00, off-season 10:00-22:00, 35F.)

▲**Samaritaine Department Store Viewpoint**—Go to
the rooftop (ride the elevator from near the Pont Neuf
entrance). Quiz yourself. Working counterclockwise, find
the Eiffel Tower, Invalides/Napoleon's Tomb, Montparnasse Tower, Henry IV statue on the tip of the island,
Sorbonne University, the dome of the Panthéon, Sainte-
Chapelle, Hôtel de Ville (city hall), the wild and colorful
Pompidou Center, Sacré-Coeur, Opéra, and Louvre. Light
meals on the breezy terrace and a good self-service restaurant on the 5th floor. (Rooftop view is free. Métro:
Pont Neuf.)

▲▲**Sacré-Coeur and Montmartre**—This Byzantine-
looking church is only 100 years old, but very impressive.
It was built as a praise-the-Lord-anyway gesture after the
French were humiliated by the Germans in a brief war in
1871. The place du Tertre was the haunt of Toulouse-
Lautrec and the original Bohemians. Today it's mobbed
by tourists and unoriginal Bohemians—but still fun.
Watch the artists, tip the street singers, have a dessert
crêpe. The church is open daily and evenings. (Plaster of
Paris comes from the gypsum found on this *mont.* Place
Blanche is the white place nearby where they used to
load it, sloppily.) Métro: Anvers or Abbesses.

Pigalle—Paris's red-light district, the infamous "Pig
Alley," is at the foot of Butte Montmartre. Oo la la. More
shocking than dangerous. Stick to the bigger streets, hang
onto your wallet, and exercise good judgment. Can-can
can cost a fortune as can con artists in topless bars. Métro:
Pigalle.

Best Shopping—Forum des Halles is a grand new subterranean center, a sight in itself. Fun, mod, colorful, and very Parisian (Métro: Halles). The Lafayette Galleries behind the Opera House is your best elegant, Old World, one-stop, Parisian department store- shopping center. Also, visit the Printemps store and the historic Samaritaine department store near Pont Neuf.

Good browsing areas: Rue Rambuteau from the Halles to the Pompidou Center, the Marais/Jewish Quarter/place des Vosges area, the Champs-Élysées, and the Latin Quarter. Window-shop along the rue de Rivoli, which borders the Louvre. The rue de Rivoli is also the city's souvenir row, especially for fun T-shirts. Ritzy shops are around the Ritz Hotel at place Vendôme (Métro: Tuileries).

▲▲▲**Place de la Concorde/Champs-Élysées/Arc de Triomphe**—Here is Paris's backbone and greatest concentration of traffic. All of France seems to converge on the place de la Concorde, Paris's largest square. It was here that the guillotine made hundreds "a foot shorter at the top"—including King Louis XVI. Back then it was called the place de la Revolution.

Catherine de Medici wanted a place to drive her carriage, so she started draining the swamp which would become the Champs-Élysées. Napoleon put on the final touches, and ever since it's been the place to be seen. The Tour de France bicycle race ends here as do all French parades of any significance (Métro: FDR or George V).

Napoleon had the magnificent Arc de Triomphe constructed to commemorate his victory at the Battle of Austerlitz. There's no arch bigger in the world, and no more crazy traffic circle. Eleven major boulevards feed into the place Charles de Gaulle (Étoile) that surrounds the arch. Watch the traffic tangle and pray you don't end up here in a car. Take the underpass to visit the eternal flame and tomb of the unknown soldier. There's a cute museum of the arch (open daily 10:00-17:30, 25F) and a great view from the top.

▲**Luxembourg Gardens**—Paris's most beautiful, interesting, and enjoyable garden-park-recreational area is a great place to watch Parisians at rest and play. Check out

the card players (near the tennis courts), find a free chair
near the main pond, and take a breather. Notice any
pigeons? A poor Ernest Hemingway used to hand-hunt
(strangle) them here. The grand neoclassical domed
Panthéon is a block away. (Park open until dusk, Métro:
Odéon.)

▲ **Le Marais**—This once smelly swamp (*marais*) was
drained in the twelfth century and soon became a
fashionable place to live, at least until the Revolution. It's
Paris at its medieval best. This is how much of the city
looked until, in the mid-1800s, Napoleon III had Baron
Haussmann blast through the boulevards (too big for
revolutionary barricades, open and wide enough for the
guns and marching ranks of the army) creating modern
Paris. Here you'll find a tiny but thriving Jewish neighborhood, Paris's most striking and oldest square, place des
Vosges, a monument to the revolutionary storming of the
Bastille at place de la Bastille (nothing but memorial
marks on the street is left of the actual Bastille prison),
the new controversial Opera House, the largest collection
of Picassos in the world, Paris's great history museum
(see below), and endless interesting streets to wander.
(Métro: St. Paul.)

Carnavalet (History of Paris) Museum—Inside this
fine example of a Marais mansion, complete with classy
courtyards and statues, are paintings of Parisian scenes,
French Revolution paraphernalia, old Parisian store signs,
a guillotine, a superb model of sixteenth-century Île de la
Cité (notice the bridge houses) and rooms full of fifteenth-
century Parisian furniture. (Open 10:00-17:30, closed
Monday; 20 F, free on Sunday; 23 rue du Savigne, tel. 42
72 21 13. Métro: St. Paul.)

▲ **Picasso Museum (Hôtel de Sale)**—The largest collection in the world of Pablo Picasso's paintings, sculpture, sketches, and ceramics as well as his personal collection of Impressionist art. It's well explained in English
and worth ▲▲▲ if you're a fan. (Open daily except Tuesday 9:00-17:00, and until 22:00 on Wednesday; 28 F; tel.
42 71 52 21. Métro: St. Paul or Rambuteau.)

▲ **Père Lachaise Cemetery**—Littered with the tomb-

stones of many of the city's most illustrious dead, this is
your best one-stop look at the fascinating and romantic
world of the "permanent Parisians." The place is confus-
ing, but maps (from the guardhouse or the cemetery
flower shops) will direct you to the graves of Chopin,
Molière, and even Jim Morrison. In section 92, a series of
statues memorializing the war makes the French war
experience a bit more real.

St.-Germain-des-Prés—A church has been here since
A.D. 452. The church you see today was constructed in
1163 and has been recently restored. The area around the
church hops at night, with fire eaters, mimes, and scads
of artists. (Métro: St.-Germain-des-Prés.)

Grande Arche, La Defense—Paris's newest attraction is
a modern architectural wonder and the pride of modern
Paris. Take the RER from Opéra or Étoile to La Defense,
then follow signs to Grande Arche. Great city views and a
huge shopping mall.

Side Trips from Paris

▲▲▲**Versailles**—Every king's dream (and many tourists' nightmare), Versailles was the residence of French
kings and the cultural heartbeat of Europe for about 100
years—until the Revolution of 1789 ended the notion
that God deputized some people to rule for Him on
earth. Louis XIV spent half a year's income of Europe's
richest country to build this palace fit for the ultimate
divine monarch. Europe's next best palaces are, to a certain degree, Versailles knock-offs.

Frankly, the place is a headache—crowded and user-
mean. Chantilly and Vaux-le-Vicomte are more likable
and easier to enjoy. But it's the sheer bulk of the place—
physically and historically—that makes Versailles almost
an obligation.

Versailles is 12 miles from downtown Paris. Subway to
an RER station (like Invalides or St. Michel) and follow the
RER signs to the train bound for Versailles R.G. (26F
round-trip, 25 minutes each way; runs every ten minutes,
most but not all trains go to Versailles. Stops are listed on

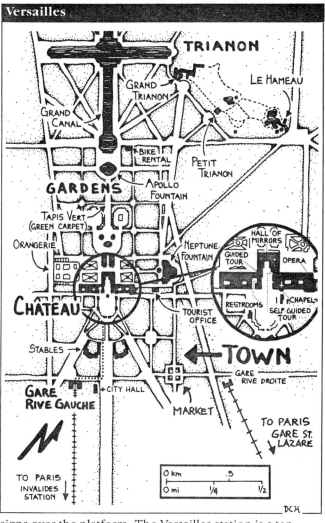

signs over the platform. The Versailles station is a ten-minute walk from the palace).

Admission is 30F (15F for those 18-25 and over 60, and everybody else on Sunday). It's open Tuesday to Sunday 9:00-19:00, October-April from 9:45-17:30, last entry 16:00, closed Monday, information tel. 30 84 76 18 and 30 84 74 00. Tour groups pack the place from 9:00 to

15:00. Tuesdays and Sundays are most crowded. Arriving
around 15:30 and doing the grounds after the palace
closes works well.

To avoid most of the pandemonium and to have your
own English-speaking art historian with a group of less
than 30 for ninety minutes, take the private tour of the
otherwise inaccessible King's Apartments and Opéra.
It leaves every ten minutes from 9:30 to 15:30 from
entrance 3 (small line on the left, opposite the long line,
as you face the palace). Tours finish at the chapel, where
those who suffer through the long regular admission line
finally start. (Tours cost 24F, plus general admission.)

The main palace is a one-way free-for-all. The Hall of
Mirrors is magnificent. Before going downstairs at the
end, take a historic walk clockwise around the long room
filled with the great battles of France murals. If you don't
have *Mona Winks* (final plug, I promise), the guidebook
called *The Châteaux, The Gardens, and Trianon* gives a
room-by-room rundown.

Many enjoy the gardens as much if not more than the
palace. The more intimate Petit Trianon is open from
11:30-18:00. Walk 45 minutes (or rent a bike in the park)
to the Little Hamlet, where Marie Antoinette played peasant girl, tending her perfumed sheep and manicured garden, in her almost understandable retreat from reality.
This is a divine picnic spot. Food's not allowed into the
palace, but you can check your bag at the entrance.
There's also a decent restaurant on the canal in the park.

The town of Versailles is quiet and pleasant. The central market is great for picnic stuff, and the cozy crêperie
on rue de la Deux Portes has a crêpe selection that would
impress Louis himself. (Some prefer to minimize the big-
city headaches of Paris by turning in their car, sleeping in
Versailles, and riding the commuter train into town. Hôtel
Clagny, near the station is good.)

▲▲**Chartres**—This is one of Europe's most important
Gothic cathedrals. Malcolm Miller, or his equally impressive assistant, gives great "Appreciation of Gothic" tours
daily (except Sunday and off-season) at noon and 14:45.
Each tour is different and costs just a tip. Just show up at

the church. (Open 7:00-19:00, one-hour train trip, hourly departures from Paris's Gare Montparnasse, 120F round-trip, TI tel. 37 21 50 00.)

▲▲**Château of Chantilly** (pronounced "shan-tee-yee") —One of France's best château (castle) experiences is just 30 minutes and 30 francs by train from Paris's Gare du Nord station. Moat, drawbridge, sculpted gardens, little hamlet (the prototype for the more famous *hameau* at Versailles), lavish interior (rivals Versailles, with included and required French language tour), world-class art collection (including two Raphaels), and reasonable crowds. (Open daily except Tuesday, 10:00-18:00, fewer hours off-season, 30 F.)

Horse lovers will enjoy the nearby stables (expensive) literally built for a prince (who believed he'd be reincarnated as a horse). The quaint and impressively preserved medieval town of Senlis is a 30-minute bus ride from the Chantilly station.

▲**Giverny**—Monet's garden and home are very popular with his fans. Open 10:00-18:00, April 1-October 31, closed off-season and Monday; 30 F; no English language tours. Nice restaurant next door for pricey but good lunches or picnic. Take the Rouen train from Gare St. Lazare to Vernon, a pleasant Normand city. There is a Vernon-Giverny bus in the summer. Otherwise rent a bike at the station, walk, hitch, or taxi the 4 km to Monet's garden. Tel. 32 51 28 21.

▲▲**Vaux-le-Vicomte**—This château is considered the prototype for Versailles. In fact, when its owner, Nicolas Fouquet, gave a grand party, Louis XIV was so jealous that he arrested the host and proceeded with the construction of the bigger and costlier, but not necessarily more splendid, palace of Versailles. Vaux-le-Vicomte is a joy to tour, elegantly furnished, and surrounded by royal gardens. It's not crowded, but it's difficult to get to without a car. (Near Fontainebleau, southeast of Paris. Train from Gare de Lyon to Melun. Rent a bike or taxi from there. Open daily 10:00-18:00. Special candle-lit hours: Saturday 20:30-23:00, May through September. 42F, tel. 60 66 97 09.)

INTO NORMANDY VIA ROUEN

It's time to hit the road—or rails—and follow the Seine from Paris to the coast of Normandy via France's most underrated city, Rouen. Drivers will reach a cozy fishing village. Train travelers will arrive in Normandy's most pleasant landlocked town, Bayeux, in a good position for tomorrow's sightseeing.

Suggested Schedule

By Car:

8:30	Leave Paris.
10:30	Arrive in Rouen, visit the tourist office. Begin Rouen walking tour.
12:30	Lunch in a Rouen park or restaurant.
14:00	Eglise Jean d'Arc.
15:30	Leave Rouen.
17:00	Arrive in Honfleur, check into hotel.
18:30	Stroll the old port of Honfleur.

By Train:

8:30	Train from Gare St. Lazare to Rouen (Gare Rive Droite).
10:10	Arrive in Rouen, walk to the tourist office.
10:30	Begin walking tour.
14:20 or	
16:46	Train to Bayeux, 2½ hours away. (May require transfer at Caen. If you arrive early, see the tapestry today to free up tomorrow.)

Driving: Paris to Rouen (2 hr.) to Honfleur (1.5 hr.)
The key to a successful Parisian exit is getting to the Périphérique (a crowded freeway that circles Paris) quickly and in one piece. Ask your hôtelier for the easiest escape. The quai d'Orsay goes along the Seine past the Eiffel Tower to the Périphérique. Follow the Périphérique west (*ouest*) to the Autoroute de Normandie et Rouen. Traffic will most likely slow you down.

   At Rouen, exit the autoroute and follow signs to Centre-ville, Rive Droite (center city, right side of the river). The most convenient pay parking lot is just off rue de la République at the Halles aux Toiles. Walk to the cathedral, where you'll find the TI. From Rouen, take the autoroute to Honfleur (following signs to Caen). For a slower and more scenic route through Normandy's delightful villages and idyllic countryside, skip the Musée des Beaux Arts and leave Rouen early, following the signs to Duclait, Lillebonne, and D-982.

By Train

Catch a train before 9:00 from the Gare St. Lazare to Rouen, Gare Rive Droite (90-minute trip, regular departures). Check your bag, then get the schedule to Bayeux for the afternoon trains before leaving Rouen's station. Spend the day walking Rouen, then catch a late afternoon departure to Bayeux (2 ½ -hour trip, possible transfer in Caen). Verify train to bus schedules for next day to Pontorson and Mont St. Michael before leaving.

Normandy

Viking Norsemen settled here, giving Normandy its name. William the Conqueror invaded England from Normandy in the eleventh century, and it was here that France's all-time most inspirational leader, Joan of Arc, was unjustly convicted of heresy by the French clergy. She was burned at the stake at the insistence of the English, against whom she had rallied France during the Hundred Years War. Contemporary Normandy is more famous as the site of the remarkable World War II D day invasion. Beautiful Gothic cathedrals, a dramatic coastline, and pastoral countryside disguise Normandy's wartorn past.

Rouen

This 2,000-year-old city mixes dazzling Gothic architecture, exquisite half-timbered houses, and contemporary bustle like no other city in Europe. A onetime powerhouse, medieval Rouen walked a political tightrope between England and France. William the Conqueror lived here, and Joan of Arc was burned here. Today Rouen

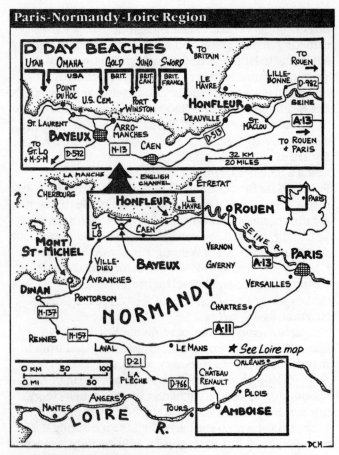

Paris-Normandy-Loire Region

(pronounced "roo-on") is one of France's most exciting and overlooked cities.

If Rouen appeals to you, stay at the ideal Hôtel de la Cathedrale (moderate, 12 rue St. Romain, tel. 35-71-57-95, in room 17 or 21 if possible). Rouen's best moderate-price seafood restaurant is La Mirabelle, across from Église Jeanne d'Arc (tel. 35-71-58-21).

Rouen Sightseeing Highlights

▲▲▲**Rouen Walking Tour**—Start at the TI (a historic sight in itself) and pick up their excellent city walking tour map and English brochure (tel. 35-71-41-77, open

Easter to September 15, 9:00-19:00 Monday through
Saturday, 9:00-12:30 and 14:30-18:00 on Sunday; off-
season, Monday through Saturday 9:00-12:30 and
14:00-18:30). Follow their route, also using the tips
below. Plan on touring the Musée des Beaux Arts, and
tour Église Jeanne d'Arc after 14:00 when they reopen.
On the walk you'll see:

Notre-Dame—The dirty exterior is considered one of
France's most beautiful, a fine example of the last over-
ripe stage of Gothic architecture called "Flamboyant"—
flamelike. The original spire was wooden. Inside, look for
the Jeanne d'Arc Chapel and the photos showing the
severe World War II bomb damage; then marvel at the
reconstruction. This is the church Monet painted at various times of day from the apartment he rented for this
purpose opposite the cathedral.

Rue St. Romain—The plaque on your right identifies
the site of an old chapel where Joan of Arc was sentenced
to death—and where her innocence was realized 25
years later. Pass the Tropical Gadgets shop, proof that
even sophisticated France can be tacky.

St. Maclou—Marvel at the unique facade that curves
away from you. Inspect the urinoir to the right for medieval plumbing. Inside, walk to the end of the choir and
look back at the stained glass framed by the suspended
crucifix.

Aitre St. Maclou—Wander all the way into this half-
timbered courtyard/graveyard/cloister. This was a cemetery for plague victims. Notice the ghoulish carvings lurk-
ing around you. It's now an art school. Peek in on the
young artists.

Rue Damiette and rue Eau de Robec—The best
half-timbered houses in Rouen (and some good budget
restaurants) line these streets.

St. Ouen—The gardens behind make great picnic
grounds. Look for the table in the sandpit (see next stop
for the best place to buy the fixin's). The pools in the
impressive square in front have made the owners of thousands of hot and tired feet very happy. The cathedral is
big and dull compared with St. Maclou or Notre-Dame.

Rue de l'Hôpital—Charcuteries abound for lunch goodies. Sample the crêpes Normandie; make sure they *chaufees* ("chauf-aye"—heat) it for you.

Palace of Justice—Gargoyles galore. At place Fochs, look back and notice the World War II reminders covering the facade. Shortly after, pass the worm bank.

▲**Église Jeanne D'Arc**—It closes for lunch at noon, so try to pace yourself and see this fine tribute to Joan. (Pick up English pamphlet describing the church for 1.5F. A W.C. is 30 yards from the church doors.) Next door is a great outdoor market for picnic fixings; it closes by 12:30.

▲▲**Musée des Beaux Arts**—Inside you'll find great paintings from all periods, including works by Caravaggio, Rubens, Veronese, Jan Steen, Géricault, Ingres, Delacroix, and the impressionist masters. Don't miss the *Anamorphose* (after many paintings by Rubens)—can you figure it out? The entry fee also gets you into the nearby ironworks and ceramics museums and up the tower of the Grande Horloge (clock tower). (Admission 11F. Open 10:00-12:00 and 14:00-18:00, closed Tuesday.)

Honfleur

This town actually feels as picturesque as it looks. Honfleur's tiny harbor, surrounded by skinny, soaring houses, was a favorite of nineteenth-century impressionists and sixteenth-century sailors off to discover the New World. Today Honfleur (pronounced "on-fluer") stands proud in the threatening shadow of Le Havre's gargantuan port.

All of Honfleur's interesting streets and activities are packed together within a few minutes walk of the harbor (Vieux Bassin). The TI is hidden a few blocks to the right of the harbor (facing the water). Pick up their handy town map and information on the D day beaches and Bayeux. (Place Arthur Boudin, in Hôtel de Ville. Open 9:00-12:00 and 13:30-18:30 in summer, 9:00-12:00 and 14:00-17:30 off-season. Tel. 31-89-23-30.)

Accommodations

Honfleur is crowded on weekends, on holidays, and in the summer. Many hotels require half pension. To avoid this common requirement, try the fine and well-situated **Hôtel Dauphin** (moderate, 10 place Berthelot, tel. 31-89-15-53) or the similar **Hôtel a l'Amiral** (moderate, 18 rue Brulee, tel. 31-89-38-26). The CH-like rooms above the souvenir shop, **La Reine Mathilde** (just off the port near the Hotel Le Cheval Blanc), are cheap and clean (inexpensive, tel. 31 89 08 50). More budget rooms a bit farther away, above the very local **Bar de la Salle des Fetes**, are a bargain—no English spoken, but plenty of smiles (inexpensive, located on place Albert Sorel, ¼ mile out rue de la République, tel. 31-89-19-69). The **Hôtel des Cascades** requires half pension, but the rooms and location are fine (inexpensive/moderate, 19 cours des Fosses, tel. 31-89-05-83). The **Hôtel Hamlein** is a simple good value, even though half pension is required. The rooms are small but clean. The owners are big and dirty but as friendly and salty as the harbor (moderate, half pension is extra, 16 place Hamlein, tel. 31-89-16-25). **Hôtel Le Cheval Blanc** (expensive, 2 quai de Passagers, tel. 31-89-39-87) is a three star splurge with port views from every room.

Cuisine Scene: Normandy
Known as the land of the four C's (Calvados, Camembert, cidre, et crème), Normandy cuisine specializes in cream sauces, organ meats (kidneys, sweetbreads, and tripe), and seafood (*fruit de mer*). Local cheeses are Camembert (mild to very strong), Brillat-Savarin (buttery), Livarot (spicy and pungent), Pave d'Auge (spicy and tangy), and Pont l'Evéque (earthy flavor). Normandy is famous for its powerful Calvados apple brandy, three kinds of alcoholic apple ciders (*doux*—sweet, *brut*—dry, *bouche*—sparkling and the strongest), and Benedictine brandy (from local monks).

Eat seafood in Honfleur. I like **L'enclos**, near the TI. **Le Corsaire** has a friendly and comfortable feel and a reasonable fixed-price menu (moderate, 22 place St. Catherine). **Au bec Fin** has less character but is very local and has a good menu (moderate, located halfway down rue Haute). For a slight splurge, worth it if you love seafood,

savor a slow meal at **La Tortue** (expensive, 36 rue de
l'Homme-de-Bois, tel. 31-89-04-93), or better yet eat
great seafood in the cozy **Au Petit Mareyeur** (4 place
Hamlein, call 31-98-84-23 for necessary reservations).
   The old harbor is ideal for evening picnics, especially
as the sun sets. Try the steps in front of the port's bureau
(La Lieutenance). **Le Paneterie** on rue de la République
is a fine boulangerie-pâtisserie. Ask for *un cigar* (chocolate mousse wrapped in pastry).

Honfleur Sightseeing Highlights
Honfleur is low on sightseeing musts but high on ambience. Snoop around the streets behind place Berthelot
and the Église Ste. Catherine for some of Normandy's
oldest half-timbered homes and interesting art galleries.
▲▲**Église Ste. Catherine**—This unique church was
built in the fifteenth century, appropriately enough, by
naval architects. The interior is reminiscent of the Pon-
derosa Ranch—wood beams fill the place, giving it a
Hoss-like warmth you just don't find in stone churches.
The exterior is a wonderful conglomeration of wood
shingle, brick, and half-timber construction. The
woodsy bell tower sits oddly across the square. (Open
9:00-19:00.) Look for concert posters.
Eugene Boudin Museum—A pleasant museum housing a variety of early impressionist paintings and Normand costumes (rue de l'Homme de Bois, open 10:00-
12:00 and 14:00-18:00).
   ▲▲**Saturday Morning Farmer's Market**—The area
around the Église Ste. Catherine becomes a colorful and
raging market each Saturday.
   ▲▲**Optional Side Trip to Cliffs of Etretat**—On the
other side of Le Havre (about a 90-minute drive) lies a
spectacular coastline. White pillars drop into the dark
blue English Channel on both sides of the village of
Etretat. Walk along the overhanging bluffs and through
the town.

Bayeux

Only six miles from the coast and D day beaches, Bayeux (pronounced "Bay-yo") is one of Normandy's more pleasant cities and makes an ideal base for visiting the D day sights. (It was the first city to be liberated after the landing.) Even without its famous tapestry, Bayeux would be worth a visit for its pleasant centre-ville.

Getting around Bayeux is a breeze. In your car or as you exit the train station, a 15-minute walk, just follow the signs to Centre-ville and Syndicat d'Initiative. (Verify tomorrow's train to Pontorson/Mont St. Michel before you leave.) The friendly TI is at 1 rue des Cuisiniers (tel. 31-92-16-26). Pick up a town map and, if necessary, bus schedule information to Arromanches and the D day beaches. (Open 9:00-12:30 and 14:00-18:30 Monday through Saturday. Open Sundays from June to mid-September 10:00-12:30 and 15:00-18:30.)

For train travelers, the logical overnight stop is Bayeux, which has several good budget hotels. Hôtel Notre Dame, right across from the cathedral, has fine rooms and a plush lobby (inexpensive, 44 rue des Cuisiniers, tel. 31-92-87-24). Hôtel de Reine Mathilde, located right downtown, has modern and very comfortable rooms (moderate, 23 rue Larcher, tel. 31-92-08-13). Hôtel de la Tour d'Argent is a bargain with simple rooms above a cheap restaurant (cheap, 31 rue Larcher, tel. 31-92-30-08). Train travelers may want to call ahead from Bayeux to reserve a room on Mont St. Michel so they can walk right to the 17:30 abbey tour.

The pedestrian street rue St. Jean is lined with cafés, brasseries, and restaurants. The best deal in town may be the cheap brasserie under the Hôtel Tour d'Argent.

DAY 6

BAYEUX, D DAY BEACHES, MONT ST. MICHEL

Busy day! You'll go from the security of your eleventh-century harbor to the stunning reality of a World War II harbor that changed the course of history, to the most remarkable tapestry anywhere, and finally to an island abbey that has become one of the wonders of the world. So take a deep breath and lots of pictures. Don't rush to Mont St. Michel; the crowds fade only after 18:00.

Suggested Schedule

By Car:

9:00	Leave Honfleur for D day beaches.
10:30	Arromanches Museum.
11:30	Lunch.
12:30	Leave for American Cemetery in St. Laurent.
13:45	Leave for Bayeux.
14:30	See the remarkable tapestry and cathedral.
16:30	Leave for Mont St. Michel.
18:15	Arrive at Mont St. Michel without crowds.
20:00	Night walk on the ramparts and stroll out to the causeway.

By Train:

9:00	See tapestry.
10:30	Rent a bike at the station and ride to Arromanches.
11:30	Tour the Musée du Debarquement, stroll the beach and bluffs.
13:00	Back to Bayeux.
14:30	Train to Pontorson.
16:40	Take the 15-minute bus ride to Mont St. Michel.
17:30	English tour of the abbey (June to September only).
21:00	Night walk on the ramparts and out to the causeway.

Driving: Honfleur to Arromanches (1.25 hr.) to American Cemetery at St. Laurent (20 min.) to Bayeux (30 min.) to Mont St. Michel (1.75 hr.)
Leave Honfleur along the road running in front of the Hôtel Cheval Blanc. Begin your day with a joyride through the once-posh resorts of Trouville and Deauville, where traces of elegance survive—casinos, pony tracks, banks, and bored aristocrats. Head for Caen, then follow signs to Cherbourg and Bayeux. Skirt Bayeux, following signs to Arromanches. From Arromanches, go west on the coast via Port en Bressin to St. Laurent, and follow signs to the cemetery. In Bayeux, follow Centre-ville and Tapisserie signs to the central parking lot. Leave Bayeux via St. Lo, then to Avranches, where you can make out the looming Mont St. Michel in the distance.

By Train and Bus
Take the morning to see the tapestry and church. Rent a bike at the gare or rent a car, and head to Arromanches and the D day beaches. See the Arromanches Musée du Debarquement, stroll the beaches and bluffs. Back in Bayeux, catch an afternoon train to Pontorson where you'll bus to Le Mont St. Michel.

Sightseeing Highlights
Caen's World War II Museum—Our route takes you right by the newest and best World War II museum in France. It's just off the freeway in Caen (Université off-ramp).
D Day Beaches—Stretching from Ste. Marie du Mont to Ouistreham, you'll find museums, monuments, cemeteries, and battle remains left in tribute to the courage of the British, Canadian, and American armies in World War II. It was on these beautiful beaches of Normandy that the Allies finally gained a foothold in France, and Nazi Europe began to crumble.
▲▲▲**Arromanches (Musée du Debarquement and Port Winston)**—The British created the first-ever pre-fab harbor here. Eighteen old ships and 115 huge cement

blocks were towed across the English Channel and sunk in Arromanche's bay to create a seven-mile-long break-water and harbor for landing 54,000 vehicles and 500,000 troops in six days. You can still see what remains of the temporary harbor and visit the beachfront Musée du Debarquement where this incredible undertaking is re-created with models, maps, mementos, and audiovisual shows (ask for English). (Admission 22F, open July through August 9:00-17:45, otherwise 9:00-11:30 and 14:00-17:45, tel. 31-22-34-31.) Walk up to the bluff behind the museum for a fine view and picnic spot.

▲▲▲**American Cemetery at St. Laurent**—This may be Europe's most moving sight for American travelers. Beautifully situated on a bluff just above Omaha Beach, the 9,400 brilliant white crosses and Stars of David seem to glow in memory of Americans who gave their lives on the beaches below to free Europe. Notice the names and home states inscribed on the crosses. Behind the monument, surrounded by roses, are the names of unfound soldiers "whose resting place is known only to God." (Open 8:00-18:00, until 17:00 off-season.)

▲▲**Point du Hoc**—This is one of Normandy's most beautiful and dramatic points. During the D day invasion, U.S. Rangers attempted a castlelike siege of the German-occupied cliffs by using grappling hooks and ladders bor-rowed from London fire departments. German bunkers and bomb craters remain as they were found. (Twenty minutes west of St. Laurent past Vierville-sur-Mer.)

▲▲▲**Bayeux Tapestry**—Actually a woolen embroi-dery, this historic document is a 70-meter, step-by-step story of William the Conqueror's rise from Duke of Nor-mandy to King of England and his victory at the Battle of Hastings. The funny shape of this tapestry makes sense only when you realize it was intended to hang from the nave of Bayeux's cathedral. After passing through a sur-real slide show, 70 meters of descriptions (in English), and a superb film, you'll be well prepared for the tapestry. These presentations are almost as impressive as the tapes-try itself. When buying your ticket, get the English film showtimes. When you finally arrive at the tapestry, rent the 5F English cassette. (Admission 22F, open May 15 through September 15 9:00-19:00, otherwise 9:00-12:00 and 14:00-18:00—a half hour later in April and October; tel. 31-92-05-84.)

✕ ▲▲**Bayeux Cathedral**—This gloomy gray church is typical of Gothic architecture à la Normandie. Notice how Romanesque (round arches) and Gothic (pointed arches completed a century later) mix outside. This was the intended home for the tapestry. Inside, gaze up to the nave and imagine the tapestry hanging there.

Mont St. Michel
Even if you're dead beat from a full day of sightseeing, the distant silhouette of this Gothic island-abbey will send your spirits soaring. Le Mont St. Michel is one of those rare places that look as spectacular when they are seen as they do in dreams and travel brochures. It seems to float like a mirage on the horizon—though it does show up on film.

Mont St. Michel (pronounced "Moan San-mee-shell") is actually an island connected by a two-mile causeway to the main land. It's surrounded by a mud flat that is slowly becoming a marshland. Stay on dry land.

Le Mont welcomes you with the most touristy street this side of Tijuana. Most hotels (and the cheapest post-cards in France) are on this street. For an easy escape, climb to the abbey and ramparts above. The TI (and W.C.) is to your left on entering Le Mont's gates. They don't make room reservations but do have handy brochures on Le Mont listing hotels, restaurants, the bus schedule to the nearest train station in Pontorson, and the tide table (Horaires de Marees), essential if you explore outside Le Mont. High tides (*grand maree*) are posted outside the TI. The tides here are the largest and most dangerous in Europe. During a flood tide, the ocean can rush in at 12 miles per hour; bring your surfboard. (The TI is open 9:00-12:00 and 14:00-18:00 during the summer; from September to February 9:00-12:00 and 14:00-17:00. Tel. 33-60-14-30. Closed in December and January.)

Accommodations

Sleep on the island, inside the walls. You should be able
to arrive late and find a surprisingly cheap room without
reservations. Still, for a good place, call ahead. You'll
notice scads of handy, but forgettable, CHs and hotels on
the approach. Most of Le Mont's hotels want you to dine
with them. Their menus are reasonable and alternatives
are few. Several hotels are closed from November until
Easter. The best budget hotel, **Le Mouton Blanc**, also
fills up fastest. They have clean and comfortable doubles
(inexpensive-moderate, tel. 33-60-14-08). **La Vieille
Auberge** has two rooms up the hill with balconies and
great views for a little extra (moderate, tel. 33-60-14-34).
I also like the **Hôtel Croix Blanche**, with some of the
most spectacular from-the-toilet views in Europe
(moderate, tel. 30-60-14-04). The **Hôtel du Guesclin**
offers good, clean rooms at higher prices (moderate, tel.
33-60-14-10). To write any of these hotels, all you need is
the hotel's name, postal code (50016), and Mont St.
Michel, France.

Cuisine Scene—Mont St. Michel

Puffy omelets are the island's specialty; at least that's
what they tell the tourists. Look also for mussels and seafood platters and Muscadet wine (dry, cheap, and white).
    Odds are you'll be dining at your hotel. If not, I like the
restaurant at **Le Mouton Blanc**. On the second floor of
the **Hôtel Croix** is the island's scenic café, overlooking
the bay and underlooking the abbey's spires.
    Mont St. Michel's latest addition is a nighttime, self-
tour sound-and-light show inside the abbey. For 50F, you
can walk through the same rooms you see on the guided
tour, but on your own and enjoy a well-done room-by-
room audiovisual show. With fires in the fireplaces and
Gregorian chants, it's a real medieval extravaganza (starts
after dark and runs very late, ask at TI).

MONT ST. MICHEL AND BRITTANY TO THE LOIRE VALLEY

This morning Mont St. Michel is all yours. Explore it inside and out. When the tour buses start pouring in, leave. For lunch, drivers will stop in Fougères, Brittany's most interesting city, for a traditional plate of crêpes. Then it's off to the valley of a thousand chateaus and your home base in Amboise.

Suggested Schedule

By Car (train travelers, see "By Bus and Train" below)
8:00	Circumnavigate Le Mont.
10:00	English tour of the abbey.
11:30	Leave for Fougères.
12:15	Lunch and short walking tour of Fougères and its castle.
14:00	Leave for Amboise.
18:30	Arrive in Amboise. Set up in your hotel.

Driving: Le Mont to Fougères (45 min.) to Amboise (3.5 hr.)

It's an easy hop from Pontorson to Fougères, where you'll follow signs to the château, where you'll find a parking lot.

Follow the obvious route to Amboise via Laval and La Flèche toward Tours (avoid the péage autoroute near Laval and keep on the N-157). At Château la Valliere, take the not-so-obvious cutoff toward Blois to avoid Tours traffic. At Château Renault, you'll see signs for the last short stretch into Amboise. Keep your eyes peeled for châteaus tucked into the forests near La Flèche.

By Bus and Train

It's a seven-hour trip from Pontorson (shuttle bus or taxi from Mont St. Michel) to Amboise with transfers in Dol-de-Bretagne, Rennes, Le Mans, and Tours. That's a lot of train changes, but the connections are good. If the bus schedule is frustrating, you can take a taxi from Le Mont to Pontorson (information at TI).

Sightseeing Highlights

▲▲**Morning Sand Stroll around Le Mont**—Check the
tides, then head out for a peaceful walk around the island
(also possible the evening you arrive). Remember the
scene from the Bayeux tapestry where Harold rescues
Normans from the quicksand? That happened somewhere in this bay. Enjoy the precrowd quiet.

▲▲▲**The Abbey of Mont St. Michel**—Mont St. Michel
has been an important pilgrimage center since A.D. 708,
when the Archangel St. Michael told the bishop of
Avranches to "build here and build high." The abbey is
built on the remains of a Romanesque church, which was
built on the remains of a Carolingian church. As you
enter, imagine the headaches and hassles the monks ran
into while building it. They had to ferry the granite from
across the bay (then deeper and without the causeway)
and get it up Le Mont. The tour takes you through the
impressive church, delicate cloisters, and sublime refec-
tory of the Gothic top floor and down into the dark,
damp Romanesque foundations. As the tour progresses,
try to hang back a bit to mingle with the past.

   Don't miss the usually excellent morning English tour
(31F, one hour). The tours begin on the square through
the Librarie (bookstore). Get there early to enjoy the
panorama. English tours are offered hourly in summer,
beginning at 10:00 or 10:30, until 17:00 or 17:30, and
about 3 or 4 times a day (10:30, 14:30, 16:30) off-season.
There are more thorough and longer tours in French
(*Visite conférence*) that include closed-off areas of Le
Mont (2 hours, 35F).

▲▲**Fougères**—This very "Breton" city makes a convenient lunch stop. It has one of Europe's largest medieval castles, complete with moat and drawbridge; a fine
city center; and a spectacular park view point (from St.
Leonard church in Jardin Public). Have lunch at one of
the café/créperies near the castle. (Crêpes are called
gallettes in Brittany and are the local lunch fare.) Pick up a
city map and castle description in English at the castle
entrance.

Brittany Option

To get farther into Brittany and farther away from it all, continue west along the coast to Paimpol and the Île de Brehat (Island of Brehat). This is Brittany at its most rugged and removed. Paimpol is a sleepy fishing village. The Île de Brehat's beauty is almost mystical. It's connected with the mainland at Arcouest by boats running every half hour in the summer and every two hours in other seasons. For a relaxing overnight on the island, sleep and eat at the cozy Vieille Auberge (moderate, half pension required, but worth it, tel. 96-20-00-24).

Amboise

Straddling the widest part of the Loire River, Amboise slumbers in the shadow of its château. By car or train/bicycle, enjoyable Amboise makes a perfect home base for exploring the best of château country.

Amboise (pronounced "Am-bwaz") covers both sides of the Loire and an island in the middle. The station is on the north side of the river, but everything else of interest is on the château side, including the information-packed TI on the river. Ask for their Amboise city map showing restaurants and hotels, and château information, including the time and place of English language sound-and-light shows. The TI is on quai du Général de Gaulle. (Open daily in summer from 9:00-12:30 and 13:30-20:30, Sunday 10:00-12:00 and 16:00-19:00. From October to mid-June, usually open 9:30-12:30 and 13:30-18:00, Monday through Saturday, 10:00-12:00 Sunday. Tel. 47-57-09-28.)

Accommodations in Amboise

Amboise is busy in the summer, but there are lots of hotels and CHs in and around the city. Many hotels require half pension.

Hotels: Hôtel La Brèche, a ten-minute walk from the city center, is a refuge with spotless rooms and a mellow garden café. A terrific young couple runs the hotel, and the wife speaks English. Ask for any room over the gar-

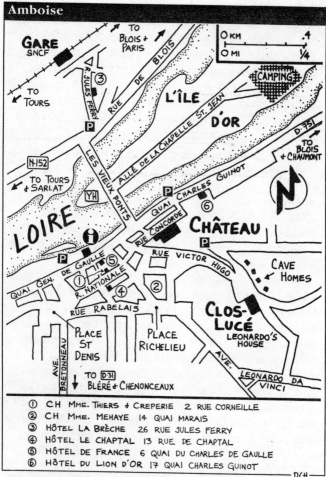

Amboise

GARE
SNCF

TO
BLOIS &
PARIS

TO
TOURS

R. JULES FERRY
③
RUE DE BLOIS

L'ÎLE

D'OR

CAMPING

N-152

TO TOURS
& SARLAT

LES VIEUX PONTS

ALLÉE DE LA CHAPELLE ST. JEAN

D-751
TO
BLOIS
& CHAUMONT

YH

LOIRE

QUAI CHARLES GUINOT
P
⑥

RUE CONCORDE

CHÂTEAU

N

QUAI GEN. DE GAULLE
P
⑤
①
R. NATIONALE
④

RUE VICTOR HUGO

P

②

CAVE
HOMES

RUE RABELAIS

PLACE
ST
DENIS

PLACE
RICHELIEU

CLOS-
LUCÉ
LEONARDO'S
HOUSE

AVE. BRETONNEAU

TO D31
BLÉRÉ & CHENONCEAUX

AVE. LEONARDO DA VINCI

① CH MME. THIERS & CREPERIE 2 RUE CORNEILLE
② CH MME. MEHAYE 14 QUAI MARAIS
③ HÔTEL LA BRÈCHE 26 RUE JULES FERRY
④ HÔTEL LE CHAPTAL 13 RUE DE CHAPTAL
⑤ HÔTEL DE FRANCE 6 QUAI DU CHARLES DE GAULLE
⑥ HÔTEL DU LION D'OR 17 QUAI CHARLES GUINOT

DCH

den. During summer, half pension is required and you'll
be glad it is (moderate, 26 rue Jules Ferry, near the station,
tel. 47-57-00-79). For a more central place, try the just
renovated **Le Chaptal**. In summer, they request you dine
in their cheery dining room with a reasonably priced
menu (inexpensive, 13 rue de Chaptal, tel. 47-57-14-46).
The **Hôtel de France et du Cheval Blanc** is very central, well worn, and run by a crusty couple who can be
forced to smile if you're persistent, clever, and armed

with alcohol (inexpensive, 6 quai du Général de Gaulle, tel. 47-57-02-44). The **Hôtel Bellevue** (expensive, 12 quai Charles-Guinot, tel. 47-57-02-26) is worth the splurge if you get a room with a balcony over the river and under the château.

Chambres d'Hôte: The Amboise TI has a long list of private rooms. In summer, if possible, call a day in advance to reserve a room. **Madame Thiery**, corner of rue Nationale and rue Corneille (dead center), is friendly and has two great rooms, terrific for a family of up to four. Her English is minimal at best, but she tries (inexpensive, includes breakfast, tel. 47-57-20-05).

It's tough to get a room with **Madame Mehaye**, as she rents to students for a month at a time, but well worth a call. Wood-beamed rooms, breakfast not included. If you don't call ahead, look for the Zimmer/Chambre sign in the window; otherwise, she's full (cheap, 14 quai Marais, tel. 47-30-46-51). Also try **Madame Jolivard** (inexpensive, 2 rue Clos de-la Gabillière, on the road toward Blère, tel. 47-57-21-90). If you're having trouble in Amboise try sleeping in the village of Chenonceaux. The excellent **Hostel du Roy** has elegant rooms (request the new section) and a fine restaurant (inexpensive-moderate, 9 rue Dr. Bretonneau, a five-minute walk to the Chenonceaux Château, tel. 47-23-90-17).

Loire Valley

The "garden of France" is covered with fertile fields, crisscrossed by beautiful rivers, and packed with hundreds of châteaus in all shapes and sizes. The medieval castles are here because the Loire was strategically important during the Hundred Years War. The Renaissance palaces are here because the Loire was fashionable among the Parisian rich and royal during that elegant age.

Loire Valley Cuisine

Since this is the garden of France, anything from the earth is bound to be good. Loire Valley rivers produce fresh trout (*truite*), salmon (*saumon*), and smelt, which is fried (*friture*). The area's fine goat cheeses include Crottin de Chavignol (*crottin* means horse dung, which is what this cheese, when aged, resembles), Saint-Maure Fermier (soft and creamy), and Selles-sur-Cher (mild). White wines are the drink here. The best and most expensive are the Sancerres and Pouilly Fumès. Less expensive but still tasty are Touraine Sauvignons and the sweeter Vouvrays. For dessert, try a mouth-watering *tarte-tatin* (caramel apples on a pastry). Be on the lookout for signs showing *miel à vendre*, fresh honey for sale.

Amboise is filled with reasonable places to enjoy local cooking. **L'Ecu Crêperie** is a fine spot to sample French crêpes—dinner and dessert. Try the ratatouille, sausage, and egg crêpe (7 rue Corneille, just off the pedestrian street, follow the signs; open lunch and dinner, but closed on weekends). If the weather cooperates, try the outdoor terrace at **La Brèche** (moderate, see under Hôtels for location). For a romantic dinner, try **L'Epicerie**. It's not as expensive as it looks (moderate, on rue Victor Hugo across from the château). The local crowd hangs out at **Café Les Sports**, across from the TI.

CHÂTEAUS—HIGHLIGHTS OF THE LOIRE

Today is devoted to the best château on the Loire. You could see many of the Loire's most famous châteaus today, but two châteaus, possibly three (if you're a big person), is the recommended dosage. This area is ideal for even the most remedial bike riders.

Suggested Schedule

By Bike (one- or two-château plan):
Caution: The ride to Chenonceau is a breeze, but continuing on to Chaumont requires strong legs or a small motor. You may want to consider turning back after Chenonceau or skipping the bike and taking advantage of the generally good all-day Loire château bus tours.

9:00	Rent bike and leave for Chenonceau.
10:00	Self-tour of Europe's most elegant château.
11:30	Lunch in Chenonceau, then pedal on to Chaumont.
14:30	Tour the Château de Chaumont.
15:30	Pedal home to Amboise.
17:00	Back in Amboise.

By Car:

8:30	Leave for Chenonceau.
9:00	Tour Chenonceau.
11:00	Tour the Loire's most awesome château at Chambord.
13:00	Lunch with view of Chambord.
14:00	Take the scenic route back to Amboise.
15:00	Wander Amboise, walk out to tour Le Clos Luce.

Timing is the key to a successful day of château-hopping. Most open around 9:00 and close at 18:00 or 19:00, and most close for lunch from 12:00 to 14:00 except in summer. If you plan to picnic, pick up your groceries this morning in Amboise.

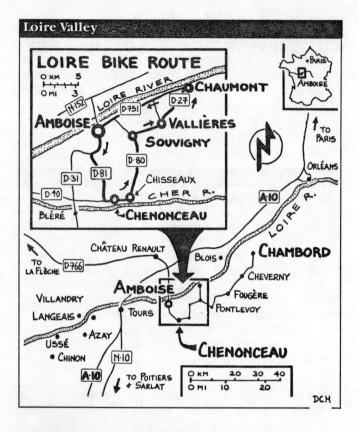

Bike Route: Amboise to Chenonceau (1 hr.) to Chaumont (2 hr.) to Amboise (1.5 hr.)

Get a Michelin map of the area and rent a bike (50F at the station or, better, at the bike shop where the bridge meets the river on the non-château side). Leave Amboise, turning left at the signal past the Shell station, and follow signs to Blère. Climb the long hill and peek at the pagoda before turning left at the sign to Chenonceau. The route is well marked except for one fork in the road, where you keep to the left. If you're continuing to Chaumont, follow the signs to Chisseaux, then to Souvigny, then to Vallière-les-Grandes. From there, you'll see signs to Chaumont. From Chaumont, follow the river home to Amboise.

Warning: This a demanding ride that many will find unsafe. Traffic is fast; roads along most of the route have no shoulders; helmets may not be available.

Driving
Follow the bike route above from Amboise through Chenonceau to Chaumont. From Chaumont, D-751 takes you to Blois. Then follow the signs to Chambord. Head back to Amboise via Cheverny, Fougère, Sambin, and Pontelvoy for a fine sample of the Loire countryside.

Sightseeing Highlights
▲▲▲Chenonceau—The toast of the Loire, this fifteenth-century Renaissance palace arches gracefully over the Cher River. Chenonceau was just another run-of-the-mill château until Catherine de Medici thought to extend it over the river. She died before completing her vision of a matching château on the far side but not before turning Chenonceau into the local aristocracy's place to see and be seen. This castle marked the border between free and Nazi France in World War II. Dramatic prisoner swaps took place right here. Chenonceau is self-tourable (pick up the English translation), with piped-in classical music and glorious gardens. (Admission 30F; skip the tacky Musée de Cires [wax museum]. Open March 16 to September 15 from 9:00 to 19:00; lunch break and early closing in off-season, tel. 47-23-90-71.)

▲▲Chaumont-sur-Loire—This place is livable, smart without being overly pretentious. Chaumont's first priority was defense—you can't even see it from the town below. I like the mix of Gothic and Renaissance architecture. As you approach the château, veer left along the path for a better view, then check out the kiddy drawbridge as you enter. Originally there was another wing on the river side, completely encircling the courtyard. Catherine de Medici force-swapped this place for Dianne de Poitier's Chenonceau, so you'll see tidbits about both inside. Don't miss the *écuries*, or royal horse house (they took this hobby seriously). Inspect the petrified footbridge and spiral staircase to the right of the stables. There's a guide during summer; otherwise, pick up the English handout. (Admission 23F, open April to September 9:15-11:30 and 13:45-17:35, July and August open nonstop 9:15-17:35, closes at 15:30 off-season, tel. 47-23-90-07.)

▲▲▲ **Chambord**—More like a city than a château, this place is huge, surrounded by a lush park with wild deer and boar. First built as a simple hunting lodge for bored Blois counts. François I, using 1,800 workmen over 15 years, made a few modest additions and created this "weekend retreat." Highlights are the huge double spiral staircase designed by Leonardo da Vinci, second-floor vaulted ceilings, enormous towers on all corners, a pincushion roof of spires and chimneys, and a 100-foot lantern supported by flying buttresses. Wander through the forest of spires on the rooftop, where you'll also find an interesting exhibit on the restoration of the château. While on the roof, look back to the rear of the château; those round corners form the bases of towers like the main ones in the front but were never completed. This is the best-value château, even though only a fraction of its 440 rooms are open to the public. (Admission 29F, open July and August 9:30-17:45; September and April-June 9:30-11:45 and 14:00-17:45; October-March 9:30-11:45 and 14:00-16:45, tel. 54-20-31-32.)

▲ **Château Fougère**—A back-door Loire Valley château, this eleventh-century fortress located in the sleepy town of Fougère is a real contrast to other Loire châteaus. Inside are fine wood ceilings and enormous fireplaces.

Sound-and-Light Shows—Many Loire Valley châteaus offer nighttime sound-and-light shows, usually just during the summer. They provide interesting historical presentations mixed in with a little theatrical glitz. Make sure an English version is offered (although it's impressive even in French) and prepare for a late night. The TI has up-to-date schedules.

▲ **Château d'Amboise**—It's more impressive from below. What remains is only a fraction of the fifteenth-century complex. This onetime royal residence turned state prison was used in the Middle Ages to greet royal pilgrims en route from Paris to Santiago de Compostela. Leonardo da Vinci had a hand in the design of the château, and "Mr. Renaissance" is thought to have been the brains behind the towers' vaulted spiral staircases. There's a superb view from atop the Minimes tower. Notice the contrasting Gothic and Renaissance styles. (27F, open 9:00-18:30 in summer; 9:00-12:00 and 14:00-18:30 in May, June, September, October; closes at 17:00 in winter.)

▲▲ **Le Clos Luce**—Pronounced "clo loo-say," this "House of Light" is the plush palace where Leonardo spent his last years. It's a nice enough home, with a copy of the Mona Lisa, but what matters here are Leo's sketches recording the storm patterns of his brain. Models of his remarkable inventions are downstairs. As you browse the models, keep in mind that he died nearly 500 years ago. Don't miss the ten-minute video next to the snack bar-café. (30F, open 9:00-19:00 June through September; closed January, 9:00-18:00 off-season; located a pleasant ten-minute walk from downtown Amboise, passing interesting troglodyte homes on your left.)

▲ **Cheverny**—At this Renaissance hunting palace you can see the best-preserved furnishings in the Loire Valley and the feeding of the hungry pack of hunting dogs (usually around 17:00). If you prefer well-furnished interiors to impressive exteriors, this beats Chaumont. It's near Chambord, on your route back to Amboise.

▲ **Azay le Rideau**—Most famous for its romantic reflecting pond setting, the Azay le Rideau features glorious gardens and an excellent *son et lumière* (sound-and-light) show complete with costumed actors on floats in the reflecting pond.

Chinon—The best view of this cobblestone town under a fascinating historic castle is from across the river. Chinon is a great town to use as a home base for visiting Azay le Rideau, Villandry, and Langeais.

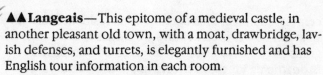

▲▲Langeais—This epitome of a medieval castle, in another pleasant old town, with a moat, drawbridge, lavish defenses, and turrets, is elegantly furnished and has English tour information in each room.

Langeais is the area's third most interesting catle (after Chenonceau and Chambord) but a longer drive from Amboise.

Villandry—This otherwise mediocre castle has the most elaborate geometric gardens and a fine "Four Seasons of Villandry" slide show.

Usse—This château is worth a look for its fairy-tale turrets and gardens, but don't bother touring it. The best view, with reflections and a Sleeping Beauty picnic spot, is from just across the bridge.

Vouvray—This is the home of Vouvray wine. Look for Degustation (tasting) signs or ask at any Loire Valley TI for winery tour and tasting information. You'll find many proud and hospitable family wineries around Vouvray.

LOIRE VALLEY TO SARLAT AND THE DORDOGNE VALLEY

It's due south into the heart and soul of France and its fine cuisine. You'll pass through some of the dullest scenery and cities in France into its most beautiful river valley, the Dordogne, and finest medieval city, Sarlat.

Suggested Schedule

By Car:

8:30	Buy a picnic and leave Amboise.
13:00	Arrive in Brantôme, relax, and picnic in the park (or take the Oradour option).
14:00	Climb the belfry of Brantôme Abbey.
15:00	Leave for Sarlat, enjoy the scenery.
16:45	Arrive in Sarlat, find your room.
21:00	Evening stroll through Sarlat.

By Train:

9:13	Train to Aubrais (1 hour).
10:38	At Aubrais, catch train to Souillac.
14:48	Arrive in Souillac, make the direct transfer to Sarlat via SNCF bus.
15:44	Arrive in Sarlat, take the free shuttle into town.
21:00	Evening stroll through Sarlat.

Driving: Amboise to Brantôme (4.5 hr.) to Sarlat (1.75 hr.)

Head for Tours on the N-152, passing under the new French bullet train route. In Tours, follow the blue A-10 signs over the river and join the autoroute to Poitiers. Bypass Poitiers and merge with the N-10 to Ruffec and Angoulême. In Angoulême, thread your way through traffic, following D-939 signs to Périgueux. Brantôme is two-thirds of the way to Périgueux.

To reach Sarlat, follow signs into Périgueux, then head toward Brive-la-Gaillarde. You'll see the Les Eyzies-de-Tayac/Sarlat turnoff shortly after leaving Périgueux. As you cross the river in Périgueux, look over your shoulder at the Byzantine Romanesque church. After passing Les

Eyzies-de-Tayac, look for the Grotte de Font-de-Gaume; take note—you'll be returning tomorrow. Summertime parking in Sarlat will give you a *mal à la tete*. Follow the Cité Medievale signs and try to park just past Hôtel Marcel.

For those visiting Oradour: Go to Poitiers, then take N-145 toward Limoges. At Bellac, cut south on D-675 to D-9, and follow signs to Oradour on D-9. From there, just connect the dots: Limoges, Brive La Gaillade, and Sarlat. Trading Brantôme for Oradour gets you to Sarlat a bit quicker.

By Train
Look for a departure before 9:30 from Amboise to Sarlat. The best route to Sarlat is usually via transfer at Aubrais to Souillac. At Souillac catch the connecting bus to Sarlat. Verify which trains make direct bus connections to Sarlat. At the Sarlat Gare verify schedules to Albi and Carcassonne before catching the free shuttle bus to the center of town. (The Sarlat station is a 20-minute walk from the town center.)

Périgord
Lush, rolling hills, thick forests, healthy tobacco fields, and seductive rivers give Périgord its exceptional beauty. It's not on the way to anywhere and never was, so Périgord lacks big cities, freeways, and smog. Exciting castles (thanks again to the Hundred Years War), 15,000-year-old cave art, and medieval monuments everywhere make this area more than just another pretty postcard. You'll find Périgord's residents uncommonly friendly and proud of their beautiful region, tasty cuisine, and independent spirit.

Sightseeing Highlights
▲▲Brantôme—This enchanting island town seems like it was made for relaxing. It tempts many to dump their itinerary. Mosey into the park for a lush picnic lunch. Brantôme's low-key TI (open 10:30-12:00 and 15:00-18:00,

tel. 53-05-80-52) is on the other side of its one-of-a-kind medieval elbow bridge. Pass on the abbey tour, but consider the personal escort up the oldest belfry in France—the first open door in the abbey as you head along the river from the TI (closed from 12:00-14:00). Superb views of Brantôme from the top.

For inexpensive French cuisine, follow the locals to Hôtel de la Poste (33 rue Gambetta). This makes a fine overnight stop, with many chambres d'hôte and inexpensive hotels (listed at the TI).

▲**Bourdeilles**—Just as beautiful as Brantôme, this town is even more peaceful. Walk across the fourteenth-century medieval bridge, admire the château view, then continue past the boat-shaped mill, through the sleepy village, and up to the elegantly furnished Château de Bourdeilles. You actually get two castles in one here—a thirteenth-century medieval castle and a sixteenth-century Renaissance château. You can tour the castle ramparts by yourself. Climb the tower. The furnished interior is worth the 30-minute, French-only tour. Highlights are the Renaissance lazy-boy chairs, the unbelievable Spanish chests, and the Salon d'Or (Golden Room) with its decorated beams, painted walls, and eagle pulpit. After the tour, walk up to the small park above the tiny church for great views. (Château admission, 20F. Open 9:30-11:30 and 14:00-18:00, closed Tuesday in off-season.)

Optional Side Trip
▲Oradour-sur-Glane, 15 miles out of Limoges, is one the most powerful sights in France. The Martyr Ville, as it is known, was machine-gunned and burned on June 10, 1944, by Nazi troops seeking revenge for the killing of one of their officers. All 642 townspeople were left dead in a blackened crust of a town under a silent blanket of ashes. The ghost town, which has been left untouched since, greets every pilgrim who enters with only one English word: Remember. (Buy the 7F English information magazine.)

Sarlat

Sarlat (pronounced "Sar-lah") is a medieval banquet of a town surrounded by hills and soft scenery. The bustling, old city overflows with historical monuments and, in the summer, British tourists. Sarlat is just the right size: large enough to have a theater with four screens (as the locals boast) and small enough so that everything is an easy stroll from the town center. Onetime capital of Périgord, current capital of *foie gras*, Sarlat has been a haven for writers and artists throughout the centuries and remains so today. Geese hate Sarlat.

Stick to the medieval city, which runs from the place de la Grande Rigaudie to the place du 8 Mai and is split by the rue de la République. You'll find most activity in the

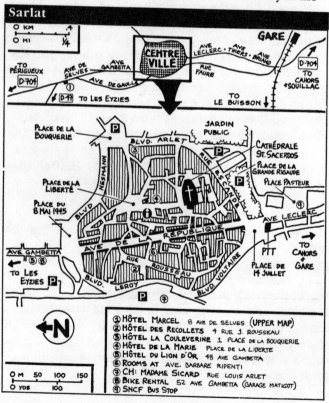

Sarlat

① HÔTEL MARCEL 8 AVE DE SELVES (UPPER MAP)
② HÔTEL DES RECOLLETS 4 RUE J. ROUSSEAU
③ HÔTEL LA COULEVERINE 1 PLACE DE LA BOUQUERIE
④ HÔTEL DE LA MARIE PLACE DE LA LIBERTE
⑤ HÔTEL DU LION D'OR 48 AVE GAMBETTA
⑥ ROOMS AT AVE. BARBARE RIPENTI
⑦ CH: MADAME SICARD RUE LOUIS ARLET
⑧ BIKE RENTAL 52 AVE GAMBETTA (GARAGE MATIGOT)
⑨ SNCF BUS STOP

slightly larger eastern half. The TI, with lots of brochures and a room-finding service, is in the corner of the place de la Liberté toward the cathedral. Pick up a map of the Old City, Périgord region, chambres d'hôte listings, and the superb *Guide Practique* booklet. (Open June through September 9:00-19:00, Sunday 10:00-12:00 and 15:00-18:00. Otherwise, Monday through Saturday 9:00-12:00 and 14:00-18:00. Tel. 53-59-27-67.)

Accommodations

Sarlat is jammed from mid-July to mid-August (call ahead and arrive early, or consider sleeping in Beynac; see below). Fortunately, its many nearby CHs pretty well cover the demand. I've listed more hotels than usual to make your room-finding easier. Try to stay as close to the Old City as possible. In July and August, most hotels require half pension. I've listed only the few places that don't and the best values among those that do.

The **Hôtel Marcel** is easiest to get to by car, a short walk from the Old City, with a very French lobby, very French staff, and clean and cheap rooms—but check closely for quicksand beds. Half pension is required in summer, but the restaurant is well respected and reasonable (cheap; 8 avenue des Selves, turn toward the medieval city at the edge of town and you'll see it on your right as you approach; tel. 53-59-21-98). The simple **Hôtel les Recollets** has an English-speaking owner and a great location on the quiet side of the medieval city. Half pension is not required, even in summer. Ask about the landlady's minibus create-a-tour day trips, if you can get her minimum of four people together (inexpensive, 4 rue Jean-Jacques Rousseau, tel. 53-59-00-49). If you're feeling medieval and don't mind paying a bit more, stay at the **Hôtel La Couleverine**. This sloppy place reeks with character; ask for the tower room. Half pension is required in summer (moderate, 1 place de la Bouquerie, tel. 53-59-27-80). Dead center in the Old City is the **Hôtel de la Marie**. Cavernous rooms and laissez-faire management make this a fun place to stay, great for families. Half pension is not required (moderate; located on place de la Liberté, look for outdoor café and inquire within; tel. 53-59-05-71). **Lion d'Or**, at the edge of the Old City, is a fair value (moderate, 48 avenue Gambetta, tel. 53-59-00-83).

Chambres d'Hôte: There are plenty within a short drive of Sarlat. The tourist office has the current listings and can call in a reservation for you.

In the summer, consider avoiding crowded Sarlat in favor of an overnight in cozy Beynac. You're right on the river and beneath a great castle. Take a refreshing river dip before dinner and enjoy the nighttime view of and from the castle. In Beynac, stay at the **Hôtel du Château** (moderate, good restaurant, address: Beynac 24220, tel. 53-29-50-13).

Périgord Cuisine

Gourmets flock to this area for its geese, ducks, and wild mushrooms. The geese produce (involuntarily) the region's famous foie gras (they're force-fed, denied exercise, and slaughtered for their livers). It tastes like butter and costs like gold. The duck specialty is *confit de canard* (duck meat preserved in its own fat—sounds terrible but tastes great). Truffles are wild black mushrooms that farmers traditionally locate with pigs. Native cheeses are Cabecou (a silver-dollar-sized, pungent, nutty-flavored goat cheese) and Echourgnac (made by local Trappist monks). Wines to sample are Bergerac (red and white) and Cahors (a full-bodied red).

Sarlat is packed with moderately priced restaurants, all serving local specialties. Find your own favorite or try one of these. The inexpensive **Restaurant du Commerce** is locally popular, cheap, and smack-dab in the Old City (4 rue Alberic Cahuet). Splurge a bit at the **Au Barbare Repenti** for the five-course menu and absorb the cozy atmosphere (moderate/expensive, located 30 steps off rue de la République on rue de la Fage on the quiet side of the Old City). Fifteen minutes by car from Sarlat is the **Hôtel Belle Étoile**, with classic French cuisine and setting. This is where the Sarlatans go for the best. Make reservations (expensive; located in La Roque-Gageac on the main road overlooking the river; tel. 53-28-36-55).

If the weather's good, hang out at the outdoor café on the place de la Liberté, particularly at night, or have a picnic dinner on the steps of the square—wine, quiche, tomatoes, and a baguette. If it's crummy out, try **La Rapière**, a cozy and happening night spot with locals. Picnics and do-it-yourself meals can be gathered along the rue de la République. For a quick, easy meal, the **café** next to Lion d'Or has excellent *salade composée.*

DORDOGNE VALLEY

This day is packed with Cro-Magnon art, fantastic castles, force-fed geese, and a rock-carved riverfront town. Today's most thrilling sight, the prehistoric cave paintings at the Grotte de Font-de-Gaume, requires a flexible schedule. Read on.

Suggested Schedule

By Car:

7:45	Head to the Grotte de Font-de-Gaume, get in line.
9:00	Get your entry time and plan your day around it.

By Bike:

9:00	Morning free to wander through Sarlat.
12:00	Rent a bike and head for Beynac-et-Cazenac.
13:30	Picnic next to Beynac Castle.
14:30	Tour Beynac Castle.
15:30	Ride to La Roque-Gageac.
16:00	Poke around La Roque-Gageac.
17:00	Return to Sarlat.

Driving

Retrace your steps from yesterday to Les Eyzies-de-Tayac. The Grotte de Font-de-Gaume (first stop) is just before Les Eyzies-de-Tayac on the left. You'll pass the turnoff to the Abri du Cap-Blanc (your next stop) a few miles before the Grotte de Font-de-Gaume on the right. To get to Beynac-et-Cazenac, head into Les Eyzies-de-Tayac and take the Bergerac turnoff. Pass through St. Cyprien en route to Beynac-et-Cazenac. Follow the signs and the river from Beynac-et-Cazenac to La Roque-Gageac. You can rent a car in Sarlat at 10 or 13 avenue Aristide-Briand (tel. 53-59-04-83 or 53-59-37-67).

Without a car, your best option is the Hôtel les Recollets sightseeing minibus. (Organize other guests to gather the minimum of four people.) The tour combines caves, castles, and geese-feeding into a great day trip (see Accommodations for address and phone). The next best option is renting a car or bike, since public transportation is scarce here. (It is possible to see the caves by train and bus, though you'd have to leave Sarlat at 7:40 and do a lot of walking, and you couldn't get back until 20:45.) See the bike route description before renting a bike.

By Bike

If you aren't going to the prehistoric caves, this is a great place to rent a bicycle and stretch your legs. From Sarlat to Beynac-et-Cazenac to La Roque-Gageac and back to Sarlat would be a dreamy route if it weren't for that killer hill leaving Sarlat. You can avoid the hill by riding from Sarlat to La Roque-Gageac first and doubling back the same way. It's 7.3 miles from Sarlat to Beynac-et-Cazenac via the direct route (10 miles the easy way), 2.3 traffic-filled miles from Beynac to La Roque-Gageac, and 7.5 miles back to Sarlat. Rent bikes at Garage Matigot (52, avenue Gambetta, tel. 53-59-03-60) or mountain bikes at L'aventure Velo (16, rue Fenelon, tel. 53-31-24-18).

Sightseeing Hightlights

▲▲▲ **Sarlat**—Like Venice, Sarlat is a museum city. There's no blockbuster sight here, just a seductive tangle of cobblestone alleys peppered with medieval buildings. Go get lost. Here are a few hints. Rue de la République divides the Old Town into two halves—one quiet and the other more developed. The place de la Liberté is the heart of this medieval town. Outdoor markets thrive on Wednesday mornings and all day Saturday. Saturday's market seems to swallow the entire town.

See the cathedral. It's musty and interesting. Be sure to exit by the door to your right as you face the front of the cathedral. Snoop around to your left through a few quiet courtyards, making your way to the rear of the cathedral. Climb up the steps to that medieval space capsule called the Lanterne des Morts (Lantern of the Dead), presumably where they buried their leaders in the Middle Ages. Turn around for a peek at some great flying buttresses. Exit

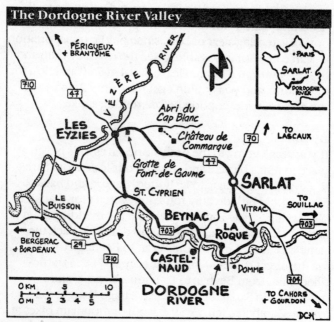

The Dordogne River Valley

right toward my favorite house in Sarlat. Turn right and
climb to the top of this street for a good look back at
Sarlat. Save some time to prowl the quiet side of town. If
you like Mayberry RFD-type museums, try the Chapel of
White Penitents on rue Jean-Jacques Rousseau.

▲▲▲ **Grotte de Font-de-Gaume**—Even if you're not a
connoisseur of Cro-Magnon art, this is a great experience. It's the last important cave in the world where you
can admire original prehistoric cave paintings firsthand,
and this cave may not be open to tourists much longer.
Your guide will explain how, 15,000 years ago, cave
dwellers used the rock's contour to give the paintings
dimension. Since heavy-breathing tourist hordes damage
the art by raising and lowering the temperature and
humidity levels, tickets are limited. In the summer, the
entire day's allotment is sold by the 9:00 opening time. If
these caves are important to you, line up by 8:15. You can
choose your tour from times still available. Nonsummer
travelers can show up during open hours and usually get
a tour within one or two hours. There's a decent café next

to the line. Buy a cave art guidebook to study, bring post-cards to write, or take this time to really talk to your spouse. (Admission 23F, opens at 9:00. Ask for an English tour. At worst you'll get the English translation brochure, tel. 53-06-97-48.)

Les Eyzies-de-Tayac—Here is the touristic hub of this cluster of historic caves, castles, and rivers. Except for its interesting museum of prehistory next to the big statue of Mr. Cro-Magnon, there's little reason to stop here.

▲ Abri du Cap-Blanc—In this prehistoric cave sculpture, early artists used the rock's natural bulk to add dimension to their engraving. Look for places where the artists smoothed or roughed the surfaces to add depth. In this single stone room, your French-speaking guide will spend 30 minutes explaining 14,000-year-old carvings. They are impressive, but their subtle majesty bypasses some. No lines. (Admission 20F, open in summer 9:30-19:00; off-season 10:00-12:00 and 14:00-18:00, closed November-April. Tours leave on the half hour, tel. 53-29-66-63.)

▲▲ Château de Commarque and Château de Laussel—These castles' heydays were over 400 years ago, during the Hundred Years War. You can see the Château de Commarque from Abri du Cap-Blanc, but you must take the walking path (down from Abri du Cap-Blanc) to get any closer. The 15-minute stroll is beautiful, but mark your way to make the return easier. You'll pass Laussel en route. Poke around the orange, crumbled walls of Commarque, but beware, it's not "officially" open to the public.

Foie Gras in the Making—You can witness the force-feeding of geese (*la gavage*). Between Sarlat and Les Eyzies-de-Tayac you'll pass a small farm with a faded sign on the barn, a small roadside stand, and a flock of fat geese. The Lacombes run the place and speak only French. Belly up to the stand and (with your mouth wide open) ask about "la gavage". Just before arriving at the Château de Beynac's parking lot you'll see signs to another gavage, which often has evening demonstrations from 18:00 to 20:00.

Dordogne River Valley—This is France's version of the Rhine, only more beautiful. Over 1,000 castles straddle the Dordogne, a testament to its historically strategic location. During the Hundred Years War, this was the boundary between Britain and France. Unlike the Rhine, the sleepy Dordogne no longer serves as a key carrier of goods. Today's Dordogne provides fertile fields for tobacco farms and beautiful vistas for tourists.

▲**Château de Beynac**—This cliff-clinging castle soars like a trapeze artist 500 feet straight up above the Dordogne River. During the Hundred Years War, Beynac-et-Cazenac housed the French, while the British headquarters was across the river at Castelnaud. From the condition of the castles (and the language), it appears that France won. Take the 50-minute tour. It's in French, so buy the English pamphlet. (Admission 25F, tours from 10:00 to 12:00 and 14:30 to dusk, usually starting on the half hour, in summer last visit is 18:00, open March 15-November 15, tel. 53-29-50-40.)

The scenic drive up to the castle (follow château signs way back) passes the goose farm with nightly gavage demos. There's a W.C. across the parking lot and a cool café in front of the castle. If you're driving, try to save some time to explore the town that cascades from the castle down to the river. If you bike here, be prepared for a grueling climb.

▲▲**Beynac**—This city's medieval light is on at night. Come here and wander the ancient cobbled pedestrian streets up to the castle and enjoy the incredible view to the river below and the floodlit castle up close and personal.

▲**Castelnaud**—Château de Beynac's rival is not as impressive, but you can tour on your own, and the view is super. There's a small museum inside (25F) with medieval trinkets and a pleasant little village below. Lots of river trips leave from here. Open 10:00-18:00 mid-March to mid-November.

▲▲**La Roque-Gageac**—La Roque (the rock), as the locals call this village, is sculpted into the cliffs rising

from the Dordogne River. As you walk along the main
street, look for the markers showing the water levels of
three floods and ask someone about the occasional rock
avalanches from above. La Roque was once a thriving
port, exporting Limousin oak to Bordeaux for making
wine barrels. Find the old ramp leading down to the river.
Be sure to wander up the narrow tangle of back streets
that seem to disappear into the cliffs. (For a romantic dinner idea, see Day 9.) La Roque is best early or at night.

▲**Gouffre de Padirac**—For a fascinating cave experience (lots of stalagmites and such, but no cave art), follow
the 90-minute, French-language tour through this huge
system of caverns—riding elevators, hiking along a
buried stream, and even taking a subterranean cruise (8
miles from Rocamadour, 40F, open April through
October 9:00-12:00 and 14:00-18:00, longer in summer,
often very long lines. Day trips are organized from
Rocamadour).

▲**Rocamadour**—This would be a three-star town if its
spectacular cliff-hanging setting and medieval charm
weren't trampled by daily hordes of tourists. Still, it's a
remarkable place, worth a look if you can arrive early or
late.

▲**Dordogne Canoe and Kayak Trips**—For a refresh-
ingly flexible way to explore the riverside castles and villages of the region, consider renting a canoe or taking
one of the reasonably priced river trips offered by several
companies in the area each summer. For example, two
can paddle the scenic 6-mile stretch from Cenac to Beynac for around 100F; or, for a little more, you could cover
the 14 miles from Carsac to Beynac. (Tel. 53-29-54-20 or
53-29-52-63 or ask at local TIs.) This is a great option for
those staying at Beynac.

Pyrénées Detour Option
Before seeing Carcassonne, you may want to consider a
few days in the Basque and Pyrénées corner of France.
The Pyrénées form the border between France and
Spain. The Basque region covers the northern part of the

Pyrénées, extending to the Atlantic Ocean. The Basques are France's most culturally independent and colorful people (forget understanding the language here), and the Pyrénées are Europe's most underrated mountain range. If you visit the Basque country, base yourself in St. Jean-Pied-de-Port and don't miss Cambo-les-Bains or the Atlantic resort St. Jean-de-Luz. The best hiking base for the Pyrénées is at Cauterets. Also consider a visit to Pau, to the touristy but still impressive religious shrine of Lourdes, and a short hike to the Cirque de Gavarnie just south of Lourdes.

SARLAT, ALBI, AND CARCASSONNE

If there were Oscars for France's best medieval sights, today's attractions would sweep the awards: best medieval city—Sarlat; best medieval fortified bridge—Cahors; best medieval fortress city—Carcassonne; best medieval fortified church—the Albi Cathedral.

Suggested Schedule

By Car:

8:00	Leave Sarlat.
9:30	Arrive Cahors, tour its fortified bridge, buy lunch and picnic here.
10:30	Leave Cahors for Albi.
12:15	Picnic lunch in Albi's St. Salvy Cloisters.
13:00	Wander Albi's city center, see its cathedral, cloisters, and colorful streets.
14:00	Tour the Toulouse-Lautrec Museum.
15:15	Head for Carcassonne.
17:30	Arrive in Carcassonne, check into hotel.
Evening	Walk around medieval walls and down to the Pont Vieux.

By Train:

7:00	Take the SNCF bus from place Pasteur to Souillac.
7:50	In Souillac, connect to the Toulouse train.
9:50	Arrive in Toulouse.
10:16	Catch the train to Albi.
11:20	Arrive in Albi, pick up a picnic.
12:00	Lunch in St. Salvy Cloisters.
13:00	Wander in Albi's city center.
14:00	Tour the Toulouse-Lautrec Museum.
15:33	Catch the train to Toulouse.
16:36	Arrive in Toulouse and take the first train to Carcassonne (trains run hourly).
Evening	Walk around medieval walls and down to the Pont Vieux.

Driving: Sarlat to Cahors (1.5 hr.) to Albi (1.75 hr.) to Carcassonne (2.25 hr.)

Follow signs from Sarlat to Cahors via Gourdon. In Cahors, follow signs toward Centre-ville to reach the fortified bridge (Pont Valentre). Look for Pont Valentre signs as you pass the station. Cross the Pont Valentre, turn left, and park as soon as you can. After a scenic riverside breakfast, explore the bridge on foot.

To leave Cahors, continue along the small road you're on. Bypass the green arrow sign to Montaubon (scenic route) and take the next right onto the N-20. Aim for Montaubon. At Caussade, take the turnoff to Gaillac. You'll pass several fortified hill towns. Bruniquel and Castelnau-Bretenoux are on your route and worth a wander. From Gaillac, a sign will direct you to Albi. In Albi, follow signs for Centre-ville and Cathédrale. Park in front of the boxy cathedral. There's normally plenty of parking there, and this puts you right in the center of Albi's pincushion of interesting sights.

Leaving Albi, head to Castres, then Mazamet, then Carcassonne. In Carcassonne, follow signs to Centre-ville and begin looking for signs to Cité (walled city). Follow the Cité signs and prepare for a severe right turn when you spot the one with a car symbol and arrow pointing right. Cross the Pont Vieux (Old Bridge) and continue up to the main entry gate. If you've reserved a hotel in the Cité, tell the policeman controlling traffic into it. He'll show you the best parking. Leave nothing in the car. Don't drive inside the Cité unless you've prearranged a hotel within the walls (not allowed from 10:00 to 18:00).

By Train

The best route to Albi is probably via the early morning SNCF bus to Souillac, where you'll catch a train to Toulouse. At Toulouse, catch the train to Albi. Check schedules for afternoon departures to Carcassonne via Toulouse at the Albi gare. Enjoy Albi, then head for Carcassonne. In Carcassonne, take a public bus or taxi to the old city or hike the 25 minutes uphill. Get the schedules to Arles before leaving the gare (see Day 12).

Languedoc
From the tenth to the thirteenth century, this powerful
and independent region ruled an area reaching from the
Rhône River to the Pyrénées. The word *languedoc* comes
from the language its people spoke at that time, Occitan,
shortened to "Oc." Langue d'oc (language of Oc) was the
dialect of southern France, as opposed to langue d'oil, the
dialect of northern France. As Languedoc's power faded,
so did its language, though a serious effort is under way
to revive it. The Moors, Charlemagne, and the Spanish all
called this home at various times. Today you'll see, hear,
and feel the strong Spanish influence on this dry, hilly
region.

Sightseeing Highlights
▲▲▲ **Pont Valentre in Cahors**—Explore this one-of-a-
kind, three-towered bridge. Considered one of Europe's
finest medieval monuments, it was built in 1308 to keep
the English out of Cahors. It worked. Poke around on
foot and climb up the central tower for a great town view
from the top. Turn left after crossing for the best bridge
views and picnic perch. Learn the fairy-tale story of its
construction. Find the devil clinging to the top of the
central tower.
▲▲ **Albi**—This delightful city's Italian ambience may
charm you into dumping your itinerary and staying a
while. The Albigensian crusades, an all-out effort to elim-
inate the heretical radicals who dared defy the Roman
church, were born here, as was Toulouse (better named
Albi)-Lautrec. Take time to stroll Albi's pedestrian streets.
Picnic in the St. Salvy Cloisters. (Cross the square in front
of the cathedral and veer right on the pedestrian-only rue
Ste. Cecile. Shortly you'll see signs pointing up the steps
to Clôitre St. Salvy.) Albi's TI is to the right of the cathedral as you face it. (Open July and August daily 9:00-19:00;
otherwise, Monday through Saturday 14:00-18:00;
tel. 63-54-22-30.) There are good city views from the
Pont Vieux.
▲▲▲ **Basilique Ste. Cecile**—Whatever you do, don't
miss this thirteenth-century fortress-basilica, a beacon of

medieval greatness. The fortifications were designed to keep the wild Albigensians out forever. The exterior is as imposing as the interior is stunning. The extravagant porch seems like an afterthought, and the tall towers seem out of place for a church. Be prepared for an explosion of colors and geometric shapes inside. (Open all day.)

▲**Musée Toulouse-Lautrec**—The Palais de la Berbie makes a fine home for the world's best collection of Lautrec's paintings, posters, and sketches. One look at his self-portrait helps explain his satirical and cynical portraits of people and life—this guy was no prize. All of his famous Parisian nightlife posters are here. The top floor houses a mediocre collection of contemporary art. Even if you decide against this museum, walk underneath it to the palace's gardens with great views. (Admission 18F, open July to September 9:00-12:00 and 14:00-18:00; off-season, Wednesday-Monday 10:00-12:00 and 14:00-17:00.)

▲**Église St. Salvy and Cloître**—This is an okay church with great cloisters. Delicate arches surround an enclosed courtyard, providing a peaceful interlude from the maniacal shoppers that fill the pedestrian streets. Have your picnic lunch here, just two blocks from the basilica. (Open all day.)

Carcassonne

From Rick's journal on his first visit to Carcassonne: "Before me lives Carcassonne, the perfect medieval city. Like a fish that everyone thought was extinct, somehow Europe's greatest Romanesque fortress city has survived the centuries. I was supposed to be gone yesterday, but here I sit imprisoned by choice—curled in a cranny on top of the wall. The wind blows away the sounds of today and my imagination 'medievals' me. The moat is one foot over and one hundred feet down. Small plants and moss upholster my throne."

Medieval Carcassonne is a thirteenth-century world of towers, turrets, and cobblestone alleys. It's Camelot's castle and a walled city rolled into one, frosted with too many tourists.

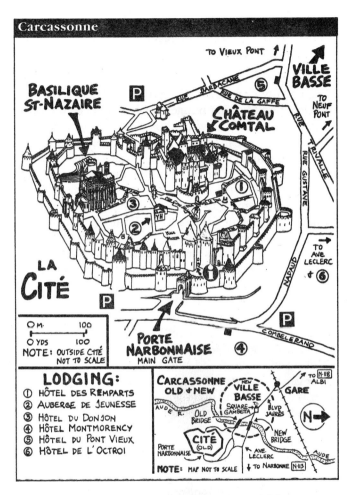

Carcassonne

TO VIEUX PONT

VILLE BASSE

TO NEUF PONT

BASILIQUE ST-NAZAIRE

P

RUE BARBACANE
RUE DE LA GAFFE

⑤

CHÂTEAU COMTAL

RUE TREVALLE
RUE GUSTAVE

①

③

②

TI

③

LA CITÉ

P

Ⓘ

TO AVE LECLERC

⑥

NAPAUD

P

O M. 100
O YDS 100
NOTE: OUTSIDE CITÉ NOT TO SCALE

COMBELERAND

■ ④

PORTE NARBONNAISE
MAIN GATE

LODGING:
① HÔTEL DES REMPARTS
② AUBERGE DE JEUNESSE
③ HÔTEL DU DONJON
④ HÔTEL MONTMORENCY
⑤ HÔTEL DU PONT VIEUX
⑥ HÔTEL DE L'OCTROI

CARCASSONNE OLD & NEW

NEW VILLE BASSE

TO N-118 ALBI

GARE

AUDE R.

OLD BRIDGE

SQUARE GAMBETTA
TI
BLVD JAURÈS

N→

CITÉ (OLD)

PORTE NARBONNAISE

NEW BRIDGE

AVE. LECLERC

AUDE

NOTE: MAP NOT TO SCALE

↓ TO NARBONNE N-113

Contemporary Carcassonne (pronounced "Car-cass-sohn") is neatly divided into two cities: the magnificent Cité (medieval city) and the forgettable *ville basse* (new downtown below). There are two equally helpful TIs, one in the ville basse and one in the Cité. The Cité TI is just to your right as you enter the Cité (Porte Narbonnaise). It's open daily 9:00-19:00, from Easter through November, closed in the off-season. The ville basse TI is at the end of place Gambetta in the opposite direction

from the Cité, near the huge French flags. (Open 9:00-
19:00, 10:00-12:00 on Sundays, 9:00-12:00 and 14:00-
18:30 off-season, tel. 68-25-07-04.)

Accommodations

Beg, borrow, or steal a room in the Cité. There are four
hotels (one a four-star budget breaker, Hôtel de la Cité,
500-950F) and a great youth hostel offering rooms inside
the walls. If you can't find a room in the Cité, hurl yourself into the moat or get a room as close to it as you can.
These listings are in or very near the Cité. Fortunately, the
obligatory half pension doesn't exist in Carcassonne, and,
except for the mid-July to mid-August peak of peak season, there are plenty of rooms. Unfortunately, there are
no CHs even close to the Cité.

The ideal **Hôtel des Remparts** is first to fill, so call
ahead. Dead center in the Cité, it has a twelfth-century
staircase, and its owner, who loves Americans, has a fetish
for cleanliness. All rooms have showers or baths; some
have great castle views and mushy beds (moderate, 5
place de Grands-Puits, tel. 68-71-27-72).

The **Auberge de Jeunesse** (youth hostel) has a great
location and is clean and almost luxurious, with an outdoor garden courtyard and a comfortable lobby. If you
ever wanted to bunk down in a youth hostel, do it here.
Nonmembers are welcome for a couple dollars extra. A
self-service kitchen and your instant family await (cheap,
rue de Vicomte Trencavel, closed between 1:00 and 18:00
and after 23:00, some small rooms and parking, tel.
68-25-23-16).

Hôtel du Donjon is now a Best Western hotel, worth
the price only because it's in the Cité. Every room has a
minibar, TV, phone, and bath or shower. Its few less-
expensive rooms befit the hotel's name, but it has a pleasant garden and a friendly bellhop. (Expensive, 2 rue du
Comte Roger, tel. 68-71-08-80.)

Hôtel de Dame is best for a splurge. It's in a beautifully restored building with classy attire, period furniture,
and sitting rooms that make you want to just sit (expensive, tel. 68-71-37-37).

Hôtel Montmorency: If it's a hot summer day, this place may draw you outside the walls. A hundred yards from the Cité, this Santa Fe-style haven sports a fine pool from which to gaze at the fortress in cool comfort. Modern, clean, and reasonable. Avoid the expensive breakfast. (Moderate, most rooms with double beds only, twin-bedded rooms are expensive, 2 rue Camille St. Saens, tel. 68-25-19-92.)

Hôtel du Pont Vieux: A ten-minute walk to the Cité, this place would be nothing special except for the third-floor three-person suite that opens out onto a private terrace with a five-star view up to the Cité. Picnic on the terrace and watch as the Cité becomes a floodlit Camelot. (Moderate, 32 rue Trivalle, tel. 68-25-24-99.)

Hôtel de l'Octroi: Here you'll find friendly owners and pleasant rooms (many brand-new) on a busy street. Avoid rooms on the street and you'll have the best value around. (Inexpensive, 106 avenue General Leclerc, tel. 68-25-29-08.)

Languedoc Cuisine

Hearty peasant cooking and full-bodied red wines are Languedoc's tasty trademarks. Dining out is a bargain here, so be adventurous. Cassoulet, an old Roman concoction of goose, duck, pork, mutton, sausage, and white beans, is *the* main course specialty. You'll also see *cargolade*, a snail, lamb, and sausage stew. Local cheeses are Roquefort and Pelardon (a nutty-tasting goat cheese). Corbières, Minervois, and Côtes du Roussillon are the area's good value red wines. The locals distill a fine brandy, Armagnac, that tastes just like Cognac and costs less.

Avoid the Carcassonne restaurants located on the main drag of the Cité. Enjoy an atmospheric meal at **Auberge Saint Louis**. Show this book and they'll give you your handpainted water bottle. (Moderate, place du Petit-Puits.) For great cassoulet, try **La Table Ronde** (moderate, 30 rue du plô, just before L'Auberge Saint Louis). For pizza or crêpes, try **Vieux Four**. With three different menus and four cassoulets to choose from, it's thoroughly funky and the cheapest place in the Cité (inexpensive, on rue St. Louis).

Picnics can be gathered at the *alimentation* on the main drag. For your beggar's banquet, picnic on the city walls. Carcassonne teems with busy, happy outdoor restaurants after dark. For fast, cheap, hot food, look for places with quiche and pizza to go.

Sightseeing Highlights

Twelve hundred years ago, Charlemagne stood before this fortress-town with his troops, besieging it for several years. A cunning townsperson, Madame Carcas, saved the Cité. Just as food was running out, she fed the last bits of grain to the last pig and tossed him over the wall. Splat. Charlemagne's frustrated forces, amazed that the town still had enough food to throw fat party pigs over the wall, decided they would never succeed in starving the people out. They ended the siege and the city was saved. Madame Carcas "sonned" (sounded) the long-awaited victory bells, and the Cité had a name, Carcas-sonne.

Most tourists lay siege to Carcassonne from 11:00 to 17:00 as a day trip from a nearby coastal resort. Avoid them by arriving later in the day, having your run of the place in the evening and the next morning. At night, Carcassonne is a cobbled cornucopia of medieval . . . .aw heck, let's just call it great.

▲▲▲**Medieval Wall Walk**—La Cité is a medieval fortress first constructed during the Roman Empire. It was completely reconstructed in 1844 by the government as part of a program to restore France's important monuments. One of my favorite walks in Europe is around the outer walls (*lices*). They're free. The higher, inner walls are mostly inaccessible, except for those in Château Comtal. Explore the walls slowly. Savor every step and let your imagination off its leash.

▲**Les Medievelles de Carcassonne**—A busy medieval fair fills the calendar with events here during the first half of August. Don't miss the jousting tournament (*spectacle equestre*) at 18:00.

▲▲**Walk to Pont Vieux**—This is an absolute must, especially at night, for a dreamy view back onto the floodlit Cité. As you exit the Narbonne Gate, go left on rue Nadaud to rue Gustave, then turn left onto rue Trivalle. (Ask: *Où est le Pont Vieux?* "Oo ay la Pon Vee-uh?") Return via the nearby new bridge for more great views.

▲**Basilique St. Nazaire**—Enter this church slowly—walk down the aisle as if in a wedding, and enjoy the colors of the fourteenth-century stained glass exploding all around you. Notice the delicately vaulted Gothic ceiling behind the altar.

▲**Château Comtal**—Carcassonne's third layer of defense was originally constructed in 1125 but completely redesigned in later reconstructions. Walk to the inner courtyard and admire the towers, but skip the French tour (no English translation), unless you've got to see the interior. Ask about English tours, usually at noon and 14:00 in the summer. (Admission 24F, open July and August 9:00-19:00, spring and fall 9:00-12:00 and 14:00-18:00, off-season 9:30-12:00, 14:00-17:00. There is also a nightly French tour at 21:30. Tel. 68-25-01-66.)

▲**Canal du Midi**—Completed in 1681, this sleepy 150-mile canal connects France's Mediterranean and Atlantic coasts. Before railways, the Canal du Midi was jammed with commercial traffic. Today it's jammed with pleasure craft. Lazy canal holidays are very popular. Look for the slow-moving hotel barges strewn with tanned, well-fed and well-watered vacationers. Drivers will pass the canal as they enter Carcassonne. Train riders will see it from the station.

Half-day Option: The Châteaus of Les Hautes Corbières

One and a half hours south of Carcassonne toward the boring little country of Andorra, in the scenic foothills of the Pyrénées, lies a series of surreal, mountain-capping castle ruins. The Maginot Line of the thirteenth century, these sky-high castles were strategically located between

France and the Spanish kingdom of Roussillon. As you can see by flipping through the picture books in Carcassonne tourist shops, these castles' crumpled ruins are an impressive contrast to the restored walls of Carcassonne.

The most spectacular is the château of Peyrepertuse. The ruins seem to grow right out of a narrow splinter of cliff. The views are sensational—you can almost reach out and touch Spain. Let your imagination soar, but watch your step as you try to reconstruct this eagle's nest. Bring good walking shoes and steady feet. A friendly, chatty woman tends the gate and sells terrific postcards (open all year from 10:00 to sunset).

Puilaurens has another impressive ruined castle, left useless when the border between France and Spain was moved farther south into the high Pyrénées. (By these directions, you'll pass it en route to Peyrepertuse.)

A car is essential to see this area. Rentals are available. To do this option, consider staying another night in Carcassonne. (If you really push it, you could see it en route to Arles and arrive there late.) To get there, go from Carcassonne to Limoux, then continue to Quillan. Look for signs to St. Paul-de-Fenouillet and Perpignan. At St. Paul-de-Fenouillet, make a left into the gorgeous Gorges de Galamus and go to Cubières. You'll see signs to Peyrepertuse; drive around the mountain and through the one-horse town of Duilhac-sous-Peyrepertuse. The castle hangs two miles above you. The road is as steep as it looks.

ACROSS SOUTH FRANCE FROM CARCASSONNE TO ARLES

After a morning wall walk, speed east along the Mediterranean coast, leaving the medieval monuments of the Aude for the Roman ruins of Provence. Your afternoon is free to explore the surprising number of sights in van Gogh's onetime home, Arles, where you'll spend two hopefully starry starry nights.

Suggested Schedule

By Car or Train:

9:00	Wander the wall and explore the Cité of Carcassonne.
11:30	Leave for Arles, picnic meal on wheels.
14:00	Arrive in Arles, find a hotel, and get acquainted with your new home.
15:00	Afternoon free to see as much of Arles as you want.
19:00	Possible bullfight à la Provençal (check with TI).

Driving: Carcassonne to Arles (scenic route, 2.5 hr.)
Use autoroutes A-6 and A-9 until Montpellier. Take D-986 to Palavas-les-Flots, and follow D-62 along the coast to Aigues-Mortes. D-58 and D-570 take you scenically through the marshlands of Camargue, past horses and roadside fruit and "sand wine" vendors, into Arles. For the best Camargue detour, turn right on the D-36 (5 km before Arles), and follow it to the Etang de Vaccares.

In Arles, follow signs to Centre-ville, then be on the lookout for signs to the gare SNCF. Just before the gare, you'll come to a huge roundabout, place Lamartine, with a Monoprix to the right. The best parking is on the left, along the base of the wall. Pay attention to signs that say no parking on Wednesday and Saturday until 13:00—they mean it. Take everything out of your car for safety. Back across the roundabout and one block away is the station (signposted), with a new TI. Walk into the city through the two stumpy towers.

By Train

Eight trains a day make the direct three-hour run from Carcassonne to Arles via Narbonne. For this schedule, the late morning departure from Carcassonne is best. Don't leave the Arles station without getting bus and train information for Days 13 and 14. Stop by its new TI. Take a left out of the station, cross place Lamartine, and enter Arles through the twin stumpy towers.

Provence

The Romans were here in force and left tons of ruins—some of the best in Europe. Seven popes and great artists like van Gogh, Cézanne, and Picasso called Provence home. Provence offers a splendid recipe of arid climate (but brutal winds, known as the mistral), captivating cities, remarkably varied landscapes (from the marshy Camargue to the jutting cliffs of the Alpilles hills), and a spicy cuisine. The locals have a contagious *esprit de vivre* (spirit of living).

Arles

"The stranger who succeeds in threading its labyrinth of dirty, narrow streets will be duly rewarded." Since these words were written of Arles in the eighteenth century, most of the dirty streets have disappeared, though Arles remains neither slick nor aloof. A thriving river port city in Roman times, Arles (pronounced "Arl") remained so until the eighteenth century, when it all but disappeared from the map. After taking a beating from American bombers in World War II, Arles has made a remarkable comeback. Today, this compact city is alive with great Roman ruins, an eclectic assortment of museums, meandering pedestrian streets, and squares that play hide-and-seek with visitors. It makes an ideal base for your Provence explorations.

Focus on Arles's compact Centre-ville, which runs from the river to boulevard des Lices. If you end up in the river or on a main boulevard, you're out of bounds. There are two TIs. The one at the train station is relaxed and has good parking. (Open weekdays 9:00-13:00 and

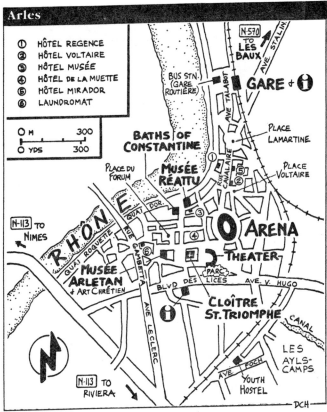

Arles

① HÔTEL REGENCE
② HÔTEL VOLTAIRE
③ HÔTEL MUSÉE
④ HÔTEL DE LA MUETTE
⑤ HÔTEL MIRADOR
⑥ LAUNDROMAT

14:00-18:00, closes on Friday at 17:00. Weekend hours
are limited. Tel. 90-96-29-35.) Drivers will pass by the
main TI on esplanade Charles de Gaulle. This is a high-
powered mega-information place with more hotel reser-
vationists than TI staff. They speak excellent English. Ask
about bullfights. (Open April to September 9:00-19:30,
Sunday 9:00-13:00; off-season, weekdays only 9:00-18:00.
Tel. 90-96-29-35.)

Accommodations
Arles overflows with dull rooms and mushy beds at reasonable rates. July is crowded; blame the annual photography festival. Directions to the hotels below are from
place Lamartine on rue Cavalerie.

Hôtel Régence is immaculate, comfortable, and homey, with new beds and a wonderful breakfast featuring homemade jams and fruit. It is family run by people who almost trip over themselves being helpful and friendly. The daughter, Sylvie, speaks English. (Moderate, safe, free parking in back, 5, rue Marius Jouveau; make a right on the first street after passing through the towers and you'll see it; tel. 90-96-39-85.)

Hôtel Voltaire is ugly and sterile from the outside but a fine bargain within—simple, small, clean rooms, all with balconies overlooking the place Voltaire (cheap; located on the corner of place Voltaire, down rue la Cavalerie; tel. 90-96-13-58). Twins of this hotel can be found next door, the **Gauguin Hôtel** (tel. 90-96-14-35) and the **Rhône Hôtel** (tel. 90-96-43-70)—same price, inferior balconies.

Hôtel le Musée is a delightful hideaway, but it's often full. It has good beds, bathrooms, a terrific courtyard terrace, and a few good-value triples. Its proud new owners speak some English (moderate, 11 rue de la Grande Prieure; can be tricky to find—veer right off rue la Cavalerie onto rue 4 Septembre and look for signs to Musée Réattu, across the street from the hotel; tel. 90-93-88-88).

The centrally located **Hôtel Mirador** (moderate, rue Voltaire, tel. 90-96-28-05) is okay, but **Hôtel de la Muette** (moderate, rue de Suisses, tel. 90-96-15-39) is better. It's slightly upscale, quiet, with parking. It's often full, so call ahead.

Hôtel Le d'Arlatan is one of France's most affordable classy hotels, with a beautiful lobby, courtyard terrace, and antique-filled rooms (expensive, tel. 90-93-56-66).

Provence Cuisine

The almost extravagant use of garlic, olive oil, herbs, and tomatoes makes Provence cuisine France's liveliest. To sample it, order anything à la Provençal. Among the area's spicy specialties are ratatouille (a thick mixture of vegetables in herb-flavored tomato sauce), *brandade* (a salt cod, garlic, and cream mousse), *aïoli* (a garlicky mayonnaise often served atop fresh vegetables), *tapenade* (a sauce of puréed olives, anchovies, tuna fish, and herbs), *soupe au pistou* (vegetable soup with basil, garlic, and cheese), and *soupe à l'ail* (garlic soup). Banon (wrapped in chestnut leaves) and Picodon (nutty taste) are the native cheeses. Provence also produces some of France's great wines at relatively reasonable prices. Look for Chateauneuf-du-Pape (not always so reasonable), Gigondas, Hermitage, Cornas, Côte du Rhone, and Côte de Provence. If you like rosé, try the Tavel.

In Arles, the restaurants and cafés on place du Forum serve basic food with great atmosphere. **L'Estaminet** offers fair value dinners. **Le Phénix** is tiny and unassuming (inexpensive, wine included; between the river and place du Forum on rue Dr. Fanton). The restaurant **Lou Gardian** is packed with locals and regional specialties (inexpensive, wine included; on rue 4 Septembre). **Restaurant Van Gogh**, just off place Voltaire en route to the Arena, is also a good value.

Picnics: Stock up at the ugly Monoprix near the station, or try the snack counter on place Voltaire where you can take away quiches, pizzas, and spinach-stuffed croissants. Ask for them to be *chauffés* (heated). The riverfront walk is a good spot for a picnic dinner.

Arles Sightseeing Highlights

Buy the "global billet" if you plan to visit most of Arles's sights. It costs 40F (28F for students), gets you into all of Arles's monuments and museums, and is valid for as many days as you need it. (Sold at all sights.) Buy the 26F Combination ticket if you want the monuments but not museums. Otherwise, it's 15F for the Roman Arena and 11F for each other sight or museum. All sights keep the same hours (except the Réattu museum): June through September 8:30-19:00; October, March, and April 9:00-12:30, 14:00-18:00; winter 9:00-12:00, 14:00-16:30.

▲**Place du Forum**—This café-crammed square is full of life, particularly at night. Don't let yourself out of Arles without hanging out here. (Always open, free entry.)

▲▲▲**Wednesday and Saturday Market**—On these days, until around noon, on the ring road, Arles erupts into an outdoor market of fish, flowers, produce, and you-name-it. Don't miss it and don't just observe; buy some flowers, sample the wine, join in.

▲▲▲**Roman Arena (Amphithéâtre)**—Two thousand years ago, gladiators fought all kinds of wild animals here to the delight of 20,000 screaming fans. These days, modern gladiators fight only bulls, and if you don't mind the gore, it's an exciting show. Be sure to climb the tower. These were the cheap seats in Roman times. Walk through the inner corridors and notice the similarity to twentieth-century stadium floor plans.

▲▲▲**Bullfights (Courses Camarguaise)**—Occupy the same seats fans have been sitting in for 2,000 years and take in one of Arles's greatest treats—a bullfight à la Provençal. Three classes of bullfights take place here. The *course protection* is for aspiring matadors and not bloody, sort of a dodge-bull game of scraping hair off the angry bull's nose for money. The *trophée de l'avenir* is the next class up, with amateur matadors. The *trophée des as excellence* is the real thing à la Spain: outfits, swords, spikes, and the whole gory shabang. Hit a few delis on the way to the arena and bring in a picnic dinner. (Mid-March to early October is the season. Check with the TI for dates and times—frequent in summer, less in shoulder seasons.) Skip their "Rodeo" spectacle.

▲▲**Classical Theater (Théâtre Antique)**—Where the high-brow Romans went for entertainment, built about 2,000 years ago, this theater held over 7,000 people. Take a seat. Imagine sitting through a long play on the rock-hard seats. There's cool shade on the grassy side.

▲**St. Trophime Cloisters and Church**—A cool, shady, two-story pool of peace and tranquillity fills this perfect square of delicate arches. Admire the church's perfect Romanesque facade and sculpture. View the cloisters from upstairs.

▲**Musée Réattu**—Here is an interesting collection of 70 Picasso drawings, some two-sided, all done in a flurry of creativity. I enjoyed the room with Henri Rousseau's Camargue watercolors and the magnetic balls display.

(Admission 10F. Open June to September 9:30-19:00;
October to mid-April 9:30-12:30 and 14:00-18:00; late
April and May 9:30-12:30 and 14:00-19:00.)

▲**Arlaten**—This cluttered folklore museum is filled with
interesting odds and ends of Provence life. The employees
wear the native costumes. You'll also find shoes, hats,
wigs, hundreds of old photos of unattractive women,
bread cupboards, and a beetle-dragon monster. If you
like folklore museums, this is a must.

▲**Museum of Christian Art**—The "Musée du l'Art
Chretien" has the best tomb sculpture outside Rome. Its
creepy basement gallery was once a Roman forum. It's
worth a quick diversion if you've got the global billet. Be
sure to go downstairs.

Laundromat—At 6 rue de la Cavalerie near place Lamartine, open 7:00-20:00, closed Sunday.

Itinerary Option: Bardou

For a unique, simple, very rustic rest, consider a visit to a
medieval retreat halfway between Carcassonne and Arles.
This sixteenth-century village comes complete with
chestnut forests, sheep, gardens, handicrafts, ongoing
restoration work, fireplaces, weekly Shakespeare read-
ings, friends from around the world, and no hot water or
electricity. Klaus and Jean Erhardt speak English and run this
fascinating retreat (cheap; the address is Bardou/Mons-la-
Trivalle/F-34390 Clargues; Bardou is 30 miles northwest
of Beziers, just north of D-908 at the town of Mons, west
of Bedarieux; telephone 67-97-72-43 before visiting).

LA CRÈME DE PROVENCE

The Provence countryside is packed with Roman ruins, interesting towns, and fine scenery. Breakfast in the dead city of Les Baux, lunch atop a 2,000-year-old aqueduct, and tour historic Avignon.

Suggested Schedule

By Car:

8:30	Leave for Les Baux.
9:00	Breakfast in Les Baux. Roam the dead city.
10:30	Watch the crowds flow in as you escape Les Baux.
10:50	Quick stop at the Roman ruins near Glanun. Buy picnic food in nearby St. Rémy.
12:00	Picnic on or under Pont du Gard. Walk across the bridge.
13:30	Leave for Avignon.
14:00	Afternoon and evening to admire Avignon. If there's a bullfight in Arles tonight, go home early.

By Train and Bus:

9:15	Bus to Les Baux (leaves from terminal at station, 42F round-trip).
9:45	Snoop around Les Baux.
11:15	Bus back to Arles.
11:45	Arrive in Arles.
12:30	Catch the first train from Arles to Avignon (20 minutes).
13:00	See Avignon.
16:30	Bus to Pont du Gard, Auberge Blanche stop.
18:40	Bus back to Avignon or return to Arles (trains run regularly).

Driving

Today's schedule is a series of short hops. Watch your map, it's easy to get off the track. To reach Les Baux, leave Arles heading for Avignon (follow signs from place Lamartine). Shortly out of town, you'll cut right following signs to Les Baux and Fontvielle. That boxy medieval

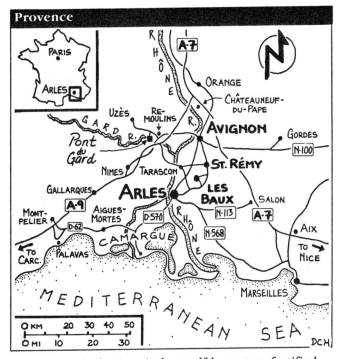

Provence

monster on the horizon is the twelfth-century fortified abbey of Montmajor. Stop for a photo; it's more impressive from afar than anear and not worth the admission. Continue past fields of sunflowers that inspired van Gogh to Les Baux an ' turn right up the hill.

To St. Rémy, continue over the hill on the D-27a to the D-5 and turn left. This can be tricky, since there are two ways to St. Rémy. Make sure that you're on the D-27a. A few miles before St. Rémy, look for cars parked in a dirt lot on the left under a Roman arch at Glanum. Park here.

Follow signs from St. Rémy to Tarascon and continue to Beaucaire. At Beaucaire, follow signs to Remoulins and the Pont du Gard. Just past the Remoulins city limit sign, follow the roundabout signs to the Pont du Gard, Rive Gauche.

Leave the Pont du Gard the way you came and follow signs to Avignon. Enter Avignon, following signs to Palais des Papes parking. Park anywhere you can by the wall.

There's also an enormous pay garage under the Palace of the Popes.

Train and Bus

Public transit is surprisingly good (and costly) in this area. With a little planning, you'll get around fine. Verify all schedule information at the Arles station. Ask about buses from Les Baux to Avignon to avoid going back to Arles. Take a morning bus from the bus station at Arles gare to Les Baux. Around noon return to Arles and catch the first train to Avignon (30 minutes). Spend your afternoon in Avignon and consider a side trip to the Pont du Gard via bus from Avignon's bus station (next to the train station). There's usually a departure to the Pont du Gard around 16:30 with a return arriving in Avignon around 18:00. Enjoy an evening in Avignon, then catch a train back to Arles for the night.

Sightseeing Highlights

▲▲**Les Baux**—This rocktop ghost town is worth visiting for the lunar landscape alone. Get out before the midmorning crowds hit. A twelfth-century regional powerhouse with 6,000 fierce residents, Les Baux was razed in 1632 by a paranoid Louis XIII, afraid of these troublemaking upstarts. What remains are a reconstructed "live city" of tourist shops and snack stands and the "dead city" ruins carved into, out of, and on top of a 600-foot-high rock. Spend most of your time in the dead city—spectacular scenery in the morning light. In the tourist-trampled live city, you'll find artsy shops and a simple church on place St. Vincent. (The dead city is open September through June 9:00-17:30, July and August 8:30-19:30. Admission 20F; tickets include entry to all the little museums.) TI tel. 90-54-34-39.

▲**Roman Ruins at Glanum**—The crumbled remains of a once-thriving Roman city, Glanum was located at the crossroads of two ancient trade routes between Italy and Spain. Walk to the gate and peek in to get a feel for its scale. Pass on the steep entry fee and backtrack across the street to the free Roman arch and tower. The arch marked the entry into Glanum. The tower is a memorial to the grandsons of Emperor Augustus, located there to remind folks of them when entering or leaving Glanum.

▲**Van Gogh Hospital**—Across the street from the Arch is the mental ward where Vincent was sent after cutting off his ear in Arles. While it's still a functioning mental hospital, you don't have to cut anything off to be allowed in. Wander into the small chapel and peaceful cloisters. Vincent's favorite walks outside the hospital are clearly sign-posted.

▲▲▲**Pont du Gard**—One of Europe's great treats, this remarkably well-preserved Roman aqueduct was built before Christ. It was the missing link of a 35-mile canal that supplied 44 million gallons of water daily to Nîmes. Dare to walk across the towering 160-foot-high aqueduct. If acrophobia is a cross you bear, carry it inside the aqueduct where the water used to run, and peek through the roof's occasional holes. Walk up the steps at the base of the aqueduct and follow the panorama signs to a great picnic site. (Always open and free.)

Avignon

Famous for its nursery rhyme, medieval bridge, and brooding Palace of the Popes, contemporary Avignon (pronounced "Av-een-yohn") bustles and prospers behind its walls. During the 68 years (1309-1377) that Avignon played Franco Vaticano, it grew from an irrelevant speck on the map to the important blob that it still is today. This is the white-collar, sophisticated city of Provence. The slick cafés and smart boutiques should tip you off right away. If you're here in July, try to save evening time for Avignon's wild and woolly theater festival. The streets throng with mimes, skits, singing, and visitors from around the world.

The rue de la République, place de l'Horloge, and Palace of the Popes form Avignon's spine, from which all roads and activity radiate. The main TI is at 41 cours Jean Juares, which becomes rue de la République. (Open Monday through Friday 9:00-18:00, Saturday 10:00-18:00 in summer; otherwise 10:00-18:00, closed winter weekends, tel. 90-82-65-11; the train station TI is also open

Sunday.) Stroll the rue de la République, snag a table and enjoy the performers on the place de l'Horloge, and meander the back streets. Avignon's excellent shopping district is concentrated on the pedestrian streets just off the place de l'Horloge. Take a spin on the double-decker merry-go-round. (A good public W.C. is just behind it.) Modern architecture has been well integrated into Avignon. See the rue de la Balance and the place du Crillon, then walk out on the wall and across the Pont Daladier for a great view back on Avignon.

Avignon Sightseeing Highlights
▲**Palais des Papes (Palace of the Popes)**—In 1309, Pope Clement V decided he'd had enough of unruly, aggressive Italians. So he loaded up his carts and moved to Avignon for a steady rule under a friendly king. The Catholic church literally bought Avignon, a two-bit town then, and popes resided here until 1403. From 1377 on, there were twin popes, one in Rome and one in Avignon, causing a split in the Catholic church which wasn't fully resolved until 1449.

The palace is two distinct buildings, one old and one less old. You'll see brilliant frescoes, well-hung tapestries, remarkable floor tiles, and lots of big, empty rooms. You can tour this massive structure on your own or with a guide. Scheduling your day around the English tour times can be a hassle, but the tours are usually good. (If it's a hot day, skip the tour and visit on your own.) (Admission 23F; guided tour 7F more. Open July through September 9:00-18:00; October to June 9:00-11:15 and 14:00-16:15. Tours in English take place twice daily, at about 10:00 and 15:00, roughly from April to September. Verify with the TI when you arrive.) W.C. in entry.
▲**Petit Palais**—In this palace is a superbly displayed collection of early Italian (fourteenth- and fifteenth-century) painting and sculpture. All of the 350 paintings portray Christian themes; the Catholic church was the patron of the arts in those days. The new special exposition room is superb for lovers of medieval art. Tour this

museum before the Palace of the Popes to get a sense of art and life during the Avignon papacy. Notice the improvement in perspective in the later paintings. In room 8, look for Mary's "neck breast" and check out baby Jesus' cocky grin. (Admission 16F, open 9:30-11:50 and 14:00-18:00, closed Tuesdays.)

Notre-Dame-des-Doms—This cozy, twelfth-century church is worth a glance on your way up to the park.

▲**Parc de Rochers des Doms and Pont St. Bénezet**—You'll like this unassuming little park. Located right above the church, it provides a panoramic view over Avignon, the Rhône River, and the vineyard-strewn countryside. Walk to the far end for a good view of the Pont St. Bénezet. This is the famous "sur le Pont d'Avignon," whose construction and location were inspired by a shepherd's religious vision. Imagine the bridge extending across to the Tower of Philippe the Fair, far on the other side, which was the tollgate for the bridge and marks its original length. The island the bridge spanned is now filled with campgrounds. You can pay 5F to do your own jig on the bridge, but it's better appreciated from where you are. The castle you can see to the right, the St. André Fortress, was once another island in the Rhône. Cross Daladier Bridge for the best view of the old bridge and Avignon's skyline. There is a pleasant café in the park.

Great Towns of Provence

Provence is famous for its interesting small towns. Try to find time to explore (or spend a peaceful night in) at least one of these:

Uzès, an undiscovered town near the Pont du Gard, is best seen on foot slowly, with a long coffee break in its mellow main square (place aux Herbes). Check out the Tour Fenestrelle and the Duché de Uzès while you're here. Uzès is a short hop from the Pont du Gard by bus or car.

Cruise up to the picturesque and popular hill town of Gordes to escape some of the heat; see what's up at the château, and act like you belong here. Pull over at the lookout just before Gordes. Continue to the still more picturesque hill town of Rousillon and climb up to its impressive red and orange ocher cliffs and caves. Don't miss the village square and the view from the church above.

Châteauneuf-du-Pape is famous for its wine. I like it for its friendly feel. Come here to taste, relax, and dawdle.

A Side Trip for Wine Lovers
Wine lovers with more time shouldn't miss the loop trip to Provence's wine country. From Avignon head to Carpentras (a fine city itself, worthy of exploration) to Vaqueryas to Gigondas to Ste. Cecile. This is France's most welcoming and relaxed wine-tasting region. Free generous samples and no pressure to buy. . . . served by folks in shorts and thongs. This a long way from haughty Bordeaux. At Les Girasols, in Rasteau, a friendly couple will take your palate on a tour of some of the area's best wine. It's well marked and worth a stop. The scenery is the best in Provence. Ideally, have lunch in Gigondas at the only outdoor restaurant in town, and end your day with an outdoor coffee under the shady maples of Ste. Cecile.

FROM THE RHÔNE TO THE RIVIERA

You're probably ready for a beach break, and today's goal is to get you there pronto. Morning will be taken up getting to the promised land. The afternoon is yours to relax in Nice. Today's key (particularly in summer) is getting to a Nice TI early to find a room.

Suggested Schedule

By Car and Train:

7:00	Drivers should leave now for scenic Riviera detour option.
8:30	Others leave for Nice.
11:30	Arrive in Nice. Check into hotel.
13:30	The rest of the day is yours to enjoy Nice's beaches, promenades, shops, and museums.
18:00	Parade along the promenade des Anglais.
20:00	Dinner in Nice's Old City.

Driving: Arles to Nice (direct route, 3 hr.; or detour via Cannes, 4.5 hr.)

Leave Arles via signs to Marseille and Salon. At Salon, you'll find the autoroute to Nice. For some of the Riviera's best scenery and most winding roads, exit the autoroute at Fréjus and head to St. Raphaël, following the N-98 to Cannes. Look for signs indicating Cannes par bord de la mer (Cannes via the coastal route). Find your favorite secluded cove, pick your favorite million-dollar home. (Caution: only drivers with rooms reserved in Nice should do the detour in July or August.) From Cannes, return to the autoroute for the final stretch into Nice. One mile past Nice's airport, stop at the TI on the right. Park in one of Nice's many pay lots. The TI (open 7:00-18:30, closed Sunday) can point out the lot nearest your hotel (prices vary widely).

Train Route

Regular service connects Arles to Nice in 3.5 hours. All sights listed are easily reached by the Nice area's efficient bus and train service. Verify schedule information at the Nice TI and gare for the next two days.

Côte d'Azur

This longtime resort mecca runs along a narrow wedge between the Alpes Maritimes (foothills of the big Alps) and the Mediterranean Sea. For over a hundred years, celebrities from central and northern Europe and Russia flocked here to escape the drab, dreary weather at home. Some of Europe's most stunning scenery lies along this strip of land. Unfortunately, so do millions of sun-worshiping tourists. Superb museums are scattered throughout the "Côte," including great collections of Matisse, Renoir, Picasso, and Chagall.

Nice

Nice is a melting pot of thousands of tanning tourists and 340,000 already tanned residents. Here you'll see the chicest of the chic, the cheapest of the cheap, and every-one in between vacationing side by side, each busy relax-ing. Nice's remarkable location, sandwiched between the dramatic Alpes Maritimes and the Mediterranean, its thriving old city, eternally entertaining seafront prome-nade, and superb museums make settling into this town a joy. Nice is nice—but hot and jammed in overcrowded July and August.

Take only a piece of Nice (that rhymes) and leave the rest to the residents. Outside of a few museums, every-thing you want is within a small area—near the Old City and along the seafront. Nice has three energetic TIs. Pick up a city map, list of museums, and excursion informa-tion. Each TI will make hotel reservations for a small fee to be deducted from your hotel bill. Nice's main TI is next to the gare on avenue Thiers. It's the most crowded, knowledgeable, and helpful of the TIs. (Open daily July and August 8:45-18:45; otherwise Monday to Saturday only 8:45-12:30 and 14:00-17:45. Summer Sundays, 8:45-11:45 and 14:00-17:45. Tel. 93-87-07-07.) The best TI for drivers is next to the airport on RN-7, Nice Feber.

Pick up their Nice parking lot map and compare rates.
(Open Monday to Saturday 7:15-18:30, Sundays
8:00-noon. Tel. 93-83-32-64.) The most convenient
downtown TI is at 5 avenue Gustave V, on place Massena
next to Hôtel Méridien. (Open Monday to Saturday
9:30-12:00 and 14:00-18:00, closed on Saturday November-
ber to April. Tel. 93-87-60-60.)

Accommodations
Don't expect Old World charm in Nice. Go for modern
and clean with a central location. When all else fails, the
area around the station has countless dull, basic hotels.

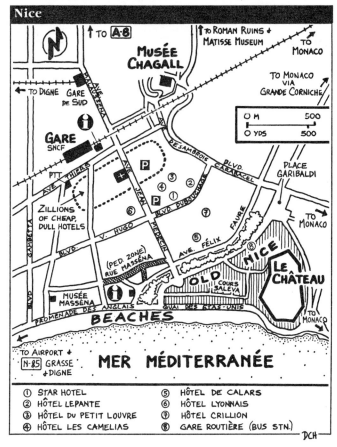

①	STAR HOTEL	⑤	HÔTEL DE CALARS
②	HÔTEL LEPANTE	⑥	HÔTEL LYONNAIS
③	HÔTEL DU PETIT LOUVRE	⑦	HÔTEL CRILLION
④	HÔTEL LES CAMELIAS	⑧	GARE ROUTIÈRE (BUS STN.)

Call ahead in July and August to reserve a room. Unfortunately, there are virtually no hotels in the Old City, and the many hotels near the station are overpriced, loud, and overrun. The best area is between the Old City and the station, east of avenue Jean Médecin. This handy location is peaceful and close to the Old City, train station, bus station, and seafront. Pick up the very complete Nice hotel directory at any TI and stick to areas 2 and 3 as defined in their directory.

Hôtel Star is a comfortable, popular, and often full two-star place, quiet, clean, modern, and run by a friendly Nicean couple (moderate, 14 rue Biscarra, tel. 93-85-19-03).

Hôtel du Petit Louvre, has art-festooned walls, mellow owners, and pleasant rooms (inexpensive, 10 rue Emma Tiranty, tel. 93-80-15-54).

Hôtel les Camelias is Nice's bargain Old World hotel and my favorite. Its owner caters to an established clientele and requires half pension in summer. . .which is a bargain. Go for the half pension. You won't eat cheaper or better (and your unfinished bottle of wine will be on your table the next night). There's a garden courtyard with limited parking, many rooms have balconies, and the hotel is located just off interesting pedestrian streets (moderate, 3 rue Spitaleri, tel. 93-62-15-54).

Hôtel Acanthe is newly renovated and has a great location (moderate, 2 rue Chauvain, tel. 93-62-22-44).

Hôtel Danemark (inexpensive, 3 ave. des Baumettes, 0600 Nice, tel. 93-44-12-04) is near the promenade and waterfront. It's quiet, clean, and has large rooms. **Hotel Mulhouse** is well located and a fine value (moderate, 9 rue de Chauvain, tel. 93-92-36-39). **Hôtel Paradis** is central, pleasant, and on a pedestrian street (tel. 93-87-71-23). **Hotel des Anges** is another well-located, friendly, and comfortable place (moderate, 1 pl. Massena, tel. 93-82-12-28).

Two recently renovated hotels of fair value are **Hôtel Beausoleil** (22 rue Assalit, tel. 93-85-18-54) and **Hôtel Nicea** (6 rue Miron, tel. 93-62-10-65). Both are bright and cheery, moderately priced, with elevators. For a friendly welcome, try the **Hôtel Meurice**, which provides a great location and an owner with a passion for plastic flowers (moderate, 14 ave. de Suede, tel. 93-87-74-93). They have great rooms in the courtyard.

Côte d'Azur Cuisine

The Côte d'Azur (technically a part of Provence) gives Provence's cuisine a Mediterranean flair. Bouillabaisse (the spicy seafood stew-soup), *bourride* (a creamy fish soup thickened with aïoli) and *salade niçoise* (pronounced "nee-swaz," a tasty tomato, potato, olive, anchovy, and tuna salad) are the must-tries around here. You'll also find France's tastiest bread specialties: *pissaladière* (bread dough topped with onions, olives, and anchovies), *fougasse* (a spindly, lacelike bread), *socca* (a thin crêpe-bread), and *pan bagna* (a bread shell stuffed with tomatoes, anchovies, olives, onions, and tuna). Bellet is the local wine, both red and white, served chilled. You'll also find the same wines and cheeses as in "upper" Provence.

Eat in Nice's old city. It overflows with cheap, moderate, and expensive restaurants, pizza stands, and taverns.

Charcuterie Julien is a terrific spot to sample the local seafood salads. Walk inside this deli, pick out what looks best, remember its name, then take a seat outside to order. Try the salade niçoise. (On rue de la Poissonnerie, at the end of the cours Saleya; open 11:00-19:30.)

Rue Droite has the best pizza stands and most local eateries in Nice. Check out **Acchiardo's** for flavor and sample the fish soup. Stop by **Le four à bois** bakery, sit down, have a coffee, and watch them make the fougasse.

For more traditional, more atmospheric, and more expensive eating, try the locally popular **Côte-Cours** on the cours Saleya, or to save money, choose a place on the place Rossetti. Even if you aren't hungry, stop by for a drink.

Sightseeing Highlights

▲▲▲ **Vieux Nice (Old City)**—This thriving old city is for real, not restored for our tourist eyes. Here Italian and

French flavors mix to create a Mediterranean dressing full of life and spice. Sniff the flower market on the cours Saleya, slosh through the fish market, hang out in the place Rossetti, and explore spindly streets of tiny shops. The flower and fish markets close at 13:00 and all day Monday.

▲**Castle Hill**—Climb here for a 360-degree view of Nice, the Alps, and the Mediterranean. Walk up and up and up rue Rossetti. Pause at the base of the waterfall for a cooling blast of air. The views are better and the souvenirs tackier at the top of the waterfall. Go all the way to the cemetery. There is no castle on Castle Hill.

▲▲▲**Promenade des Anglais**—There's something for everyone along this seafront circus. Watch the Europeans at play, admire the azure Mediterranean, anchor yourself in one of the blue chairs, and prop your feet up on the made-to-order guardrail. Ahhh, the Riviera! Join the evening parade of tans along the promenade.

Beaches of Nice—Where the jet set lies on the rocks. After some time settling into the pebbles, you can play beach volleyball, Ping-Pong, or boules, rent paddle boats, jet skis, or wind surfers, explore ways to use your zoom lens as a telescope, or snooze on comfy beach-beds with end tables. Before you head off in search of sandy beaches, try it on the rocks.

▲▲**Musée National Marc Chagall**—Even if you're suspicious of modern art, this museum is a joy. A 15-minute walk from the station or bus #15, a wonderful selection of Chagall's work is beautifully displayed according to the artist's design. The brilliant blues and reds of his large oil paintings are exhilarating, as are the spiritual and folk themes. Don't miss the stained-glass windows of the auditorium. The small guidebook has a great rundown on each meaningful painting. (Admission 22F, 16F off-season; open July to September 10:00-19:00; off-season 10:00-12:30 and 14:00-17:30, closed Tuesdays. To get there, leaving the station, walk left along avenue Thiers for about 8 blocks.)

Nice Municipal Museums—The city of Nice has established 12 free, interesting museums with themes ranging from archaeological to naval and Renaissance to its impressive new modern art museum. Get a Nice museum brochure at the TI for descriptions and current hours. My favorite is the Nice knickknack Musée Masséna, housed in a beautiful mansion across from the promenade des Anglais and full of historical Nice paraphernalia (65 rue de France).

Russian Cathedral—If you've never been to the U.S.S.R., this is worth a detour. Situated between two tennis courts, the stunning onion domes seem proud, but odd, on the racy Riveria. (12F, no shorts, open 9:00-12:00 and 14:30-17:00; in July and August, open until 20:00. At 17, boulevard du Tsarevitch.)

Shopping Streets—The pedestrian streets of rue Masséna are packed with tourists, uninteresting cafés, and overpriced boutiques. Window-shop the expensive boutiques and sift through the fascinating crowds. The dime-a-dozen cafés are well stocked with bad food.

Nice Tidbits: Tune in to Sunshine Radio, 97.1, for some familiar language and music and a bit of the British and U.S. expatriate community at work. Drop into the English-speaking Riviera Bookshop for something to read on the beach (10 rue Chauvain). Self-service laundromats are everywhere in Nice—ask your hôtelier.

BEACHES, CASINOS, AND PICASSO ON THE CÔTE D'AZUR

This day is yours to do as much or as little as you like. I've described three very different day trips: luxurious Monte Carlo, the beachy, artsy port town of Antibes, and the inland Alpes Maritimes towns of St. Paul and Vence. They're all interesting, but so is Nice. Depending on your interests and your need for a rest, why not take the morning to discover one of these places, then return for an afternoon of relaxation in Nice?

Suggested Schedule

By Train (for drivers, too)

10:00	Bus to Monte Carlo, see changing of guard, picnic, and visit casino.
14:00	Train to Antibes for Picasso museum, the old town, and its beach.
17:00	Train back to Nice.

Nice Day Trips
Nice is perfectly located for exploring the Côte d'Azur's alluring sights. You could drive, but I'd park in Nice and relax on the buses and trains. Buses depart from the Gare Routière, which fronts on the Old City, and trains leave from the main station on avenue Thiers. Buses or trains run regularly to all of the following day trip sights.

Monte Carlo (half day)—Monte Carlo is still a dazzling place in spite of overdevelopment and crass commercialization. The ride here and back alone will make you glad you came. This minuscule country is a haven for the rich and famous, who pay minimal taxes as Monaco residents. Stroll the streets. Count the counts and Rolls-Royces around the four-star hotels near the casino. Strut inside the lavish casino as if you owned the place. Anyone can get as far as the one-armed bandits and roulette tables; you'll have to be 21, and pay 50F to get into serious card

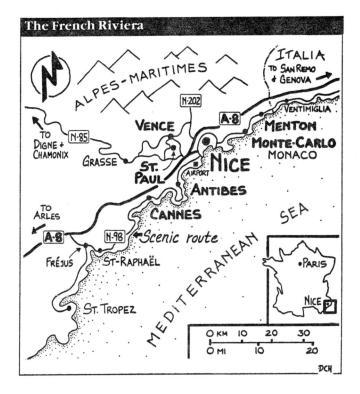

The French Riviera

games. After watching the almost comical changing of the guard, wander the old city, buy the local Pan Bagna and a drink for a picnic in the park overlooking the Mediterranean near the aquarium. Then walk down along the harbor and up to the casino. The nearby Musée de l'Océanographie (Cousteau Aquarium) is the largest of its kind in the world (50F). The Monte Carlo story film (35F, 9:30-19:00, below the Museum of Oceanography) gives an interesting English-language history of this tiny country. For city information, call the TI at 93-50-60-88. To get two dreamy perspectives of the spectacular coast between Nice and Monte Carlo, take the bus via the Moyenne corniche (middle road) and return on train or bus via the Basse corniche (lower road). A public bus connects Monte Carlo's station and palace.

Cannes—Its sister city is Beverly Hills.

Menton—Just a few minutes by train from Monaco or
Nice, Menton is a relatively quiet and relaxing spa and
beach town (TI tel. 93-57-57-00).
Antibes (half day, 32F round-trip by train)—For a
pleasant, sandy cove, an interesting old town, and a fine
Picasso collection, visit Antibes. In the summer, the main
beaches are jammed, though the smaller harbor adjacent
to the *plage* (beach) de la Gravette isn't too overrun.
Antibe's glamorous port glistens with luxurious yachts
and quaint fishing boats. You're welcome to browse. The
Old City of Antibes is quaint in a sandy-sophisticated
way. A fine daily market bustles until 13:00. The Musée
Grimaldi, which houses numerous Picassos, is set beautifully where the Old City meets the sea (look for signs
from the Old City). You'll understand why Picasso liked
working here. (Open July-September 10:00-12:00 and
15:00-19:00; October-June 10:00-12:00 and 14:00-18:00.
Closed Tuesday, 20F.) TI at 11, place de Gaulle, tel.
93-33-95-64.
St. Paul and St.-Paul-de-Vence (half day)—If you
prefer hill towns to beaches, head for St. Paul and Vence
(bus from Gare Routière, 15F). Unless you go early, you'll
escape only some of the heat and none of the crowds.
The 30-minute ride brings great climatic and cultural
changes. St. Paul is part cozy medieval hill town and part
local artist shopping mall. It is pleasantly artsy but gets
swamped with tour buses. Dodge the crowds by arriving
early or late or by meandering into St. Paul's quieter
streets. Wander far to enjoy the panoramic views. TI tel.
93-32-86-95.

The prestigious, far-out, high-priced Fondation Maeght
art gallery is a 10-minute steep walk uphill. If ever modern art could appeal to you, this would be the place. Its
enigmatic art is shuffled holistically among pleasant gardens and stunning views. (Admission 45F, open July to
September 10:00-19:00; October to June 10:00-12:30 and
14:30-18:00. Tel. 93-32-81-63.)

The hill town of Vence is less claustrophobic, spreading
St. Paul's crowds over a larger and more interesting city.

Vence bubbles with workaday and tourist activity. Catch the daily market (ends at 12:30), and don't miss the small church with its Chagall mosaic and moving Chapelle St. Sacrament. Matisse's much raved about Chapelle du Rosaire (one mile from Vence toward St. Jeannet, taxi or walk) seems overrated, though the yellow, blue, and green filtered sunlight does a cheery dance in stark contrast to the gloomy tile sketches. (Donation requested. Open only on Tuesday and Thursday 10:00-11:30 and 14:30-17:30 and Friday 14:30-17:00, plus summer Wednesday and Saturday afternoons, closed November through December 15, or open by appointment; tel. 93-58-03-26. Vence TI on place du Grand Jardin, tel. 93-58-06-38.)

Villefranche sur Mer, a small, uncrowded port village that may remind you more of Italy than France, is a fine escape from the noise and crowds of Nice. Come here for dinner and try the excellent café just below the station on the beach. Then wander into the village for ice cream. Find hidden squares and the *rue obscure*. (Only 10 minutes by train from Nice. Trains run regularly, but check the return schedule—usually only 21:40 or midnight.)

FROM RIVIERA PALM TREES TO ALPINE SNOWBALLS

Dive headlong into the dramatic French Alps today. It's a long and winding route by train or car, but the scenery is nonstop spectacular, and the destination is worth the effort. You'll pass through Jean-Claude Killy's Grenoble and skirt the mountain resort of Albertville, site of the 1992 winter Olympics.

Suggested Schedule by Car	
8:00	Leave Nice and travel north into the Alps.
17:00	Arrive in Chamonix. Find your hotel. Fondue for dinner?

Driving: Nice to Digne (3 hr.) to Grenoble (3 hr.) to Chamonix (2 hr.)

Get an early start. Leave Nice following signs to Grasse and Digne. From Digne, the route is straightforward to Sisteron and Grenoble. Between Grenoble and Chamonix, you can take the relaxing, less scenic autoroute via Annecy or the more scenic but windy local N-90 to N-212 route via Albertville, Ugine, and St. Gervais-les-Bain. Both routes take about the same time. I'd lunch in Sisteron and use the autoroute after Grenoble.

   Driving detour via Europe's Grand Canyon du Verdon: Europe's most magnificent canyon (according to the French) lies between Grasse and Digne. Take the D-952 turnoff at Castellane to Rougon and plan on several hours (at least) to explore the 15-mile-long canyon. It's over 2,000 feet deep and only a few feet wide at its narrowest. Follow the "Corniche sublime" route. Overnight in Castellane, Digne, or Sisteron.

By Train

You have two choices. I suggest relaxing in Nice for the day and taking the night train (about 20:30), arriving in

Chamonix by about 10:00 the next morning. For the all-day scenic option, leave Nice around 6:30 and arrive at Chamonix by about 19:00. Verify at Nice Gare. Some trains go via St. Gervais.

Alpes-Savoie

Savoie is the mountainous area that lies in the northern tier of the French Alps (the Alpes-Dauphiné lie to the south). In the eleventh century, Savoie was a powerful region with borders stretching down to the Riviera and out to the Rhône. Today, it's France's mountain sports capital with Europe's highest point, Mont Blanc, as its centerpiece. Savoie didn't become a part of France until 1860 and still seems like it should have gone Swiss instead.

Chamonix

With gondolas, chair lifts, rackrailways, and myriad trails waiting to take you high into alpine heaven, the tourist-filled resort of Chamonix makes a perfect base for your Alps exploration.

Chamonix (pronounced "Sham-oh-nee") is actually ten small villages nestled in the valley below Mont Blanc. The largest village is also called Chamonix. It's the best served by mountain lifts. Every place we'll visit is an "isn't it great to be alive" walk, chair lift, gondola, or train ride away. Chamonix's small pedestrian zone is the center, though you'll find most activity along the rue du Docteur Paccard. To the east is the Mont Blanc range. To the west is the Aiguilles Rouges chain. The excellent TI provides hotel and hiking hut reservations, a map of the town and valley listing restaurants and hotels, and an essential 20F hiking mountain map called "Carte des Sentiers." (Located one block west of rue du Docteur Paccard and the pedestrian area, on the place de l'Église—you'll see a green church spire. Open July and August 8:30-19:30; October to June 8:30-12:30 and 14:00-19:00; tel. 50-53-00-24 or 50-53-23-33 for hotel reservations.)

An essential stop for serious hikers is the Office de Haute Montagne (Office of the High Mountains), across

from the TI on the third floor of the building marked
"Maison de la Montagne" next to the church. The eager
staff speaks some English and will gladly give you their
opinions on the most interesting hikes (*randonnées
pédestres*) in the area. More important, they have up-to-
date weather and trail condition reports. (Tel. 50-23-22-08.)

Accommodations

Reasonable one- and two-star hotels and cheap dormlike
chalets abound. With the helpful TI, you can find budget
accommodations anytime. July 20 through August 16 is
most difficult. My favorite Chamonix experience is to spend
a night high in the mountains at a *refuge* (hiking hut).
Expect major crowds in the summer. If it's too much,
consider staying in one of the smaller, quieter towns up
the valley toward Switzerland.

Hôtel de l'Arve has fine view rooms right on the Arve
River, overlooking Mont Blanc, or cheaper rooms without the view, W.C.'s and showers. Friendly but jammed in
the summer, it's still worth a try (moderate, located
between the Arve River and rue Joseph Valliot, tel.
50-53-02-31, plenty of parking).

Hôtel le Chamonix (moderate, 58 place de l'Eglise,
across from the TI, tel. 50-53-11-07) is clean and central.

Hotel Au Bon Coin (moderate, 80 ave. L'Aiguille du
Midi, tel. 50-53-15-67) has great views and a balcony for
each room. **Hotel Touring** (moderate, rue Joseph Vallot,
left of supermarket, tel. 50-53-59-18) is British-owned
with friendly service and big rooms (get one off the
street). **Hotel Chantel** (moderate, 391 route des Pecles,
tel. 50-53-11-07) is quiet, outside of town, and offers the
feeling of a Swiss chalet.

Hôtel Asia, the pinkest building in town (inexpensive/
moderate, on rue du Dr. Paccard, tel. 50-55-99-25) is a
good last resort.

Hôtel Gourmets-Italy is well located and worth the
splurge (expensive, direction Pantalacci, tel. 50-53-01-38).

For cheaper dormlike accommodations, about a ten-
minute walk from the town center, try **Les Grands
Charmoz**. Fifty-two francs buys a bunk and sheet, free

showers, and a kitchen available for do-it-yourselfers.
They also have some good, clean doubles with kitchen
privileges as well as apartments upstairs (cheap; 468 chemin
des Cristalliers; turn right out of the station and cross
over the tracks at the Hôtel Albert and then turn left; tel.
50-53-45-57). The **Chalet Ski Station** also has bunks,
but no doubles (cheap, next to the Brevent téléphérique,
a five-minute hike up from the TIs, tel. 50-53-20-25), as
does **La Montagne** (just a few kilometers up the valley
from Chamonix, tel. 50-53-11-60).

Chamonix's youth hostel was formerly the barracks for
the diggers of the Mont Blanc tunnel. Well run and cheap,
it sells substantially discounted lift tickets for the most
expensive lifts in the valley. Hostel members are welcome
to drop in and buy these discounted tickets even if they
sleep elsewhere (55F per dorm bed, 5-minute walk from
the base of the Aiguille du Midi lift or a ten-minute walk
up from the Les Pèlerins Station, 2 kilometers below
Chamonix, tel. 50-53-14-52).

Refuges: The French have the perfect answer for
hikers who don't want to pack tents, sleeping bags,
stoves, and food: refuges. For 45F to 100F, you can sleep
on bunks high in the peaceful mountains. Bring your
own food or let the guardian cook your dinner and
breakfast (75F for dinner and 35F for breakfast). The
Office de Haute Montagne can explain your options, and
the TI will make your refuge reservations. Most refuges
are located an easy walk from a lift station and are open
from mid-June to mid-September. Comfort ranges from
very basic to downright luxurious.

The campground with the best views in the valley is a
20-minute streamside walk toward Les Praz down rue
Joseph Vallot. Look for **Camping Les Rosières** (tel.
50-53-10-42). They also rent fully equipped trailers.

Savoie Cuisine
This is mountain country cuisine. Robust and hearty, it
borrows much from the Swiss. *Fondue savoyarde*
(melted cheese and wine), *raclette* (chunks of semi-
melted cheese served with potatoes, pickles, sausage, and
bread), Bresse chicken (the best chicken in France), *mor-*

teau (smoked pork sausage), *gratin savoyarde* (a potato dish using cream, cheese, and garlic), and freshly caught fish are the specialties. Local cheeses are Morbier (look for a charcoal streak down the middle), Comté (like Gruyère), Beaufort (aged for two years, hard and strong), Reblochon (mild and creamy), and Tomme de Savoie (semihard and mild). Evian water comes from Savoie, as does Chartreuse liqueur. Vin de Savoie and Crépy are two of the area's surprisingly good white wines.

While Chamonix, like any mountain resort, has its share of bad-food, bad-price restaurants, there are a few good values to be found.

Le Fer à Cheval is famous as the place for fondue and raclette in Chamonix (inexpensive, on rue Whymper near place Mont Blanc). I prefer the low-key **Restaurant La Cascade-Chez Jeannot** next door. If dipping bread into hot gurgling cheese isn't your idea of haute cuisine, try **Crêperie Le Sabot** on allée Recteur Payot for good crêpes and omelets. For simple, cheap fare, you'll find several good places on the rue Joseph Vallot. Look for **Brasserie des Spors**, a souvenir of old Chamonix with wood tables and old photos, and the classy self-service cafeteria **Le Grilland**.

R'mize de Ravanel before Argentiere Les Grassonnets, 6 kilometers north of Chamonix, has great moderately priced dinners.

La Caboulé, next to the Le Brevent téléphérique, is a funky eatery with great omelets and an unbeatable view from its outdoor tables.

Restaurant Impossible (the nickname of its popular local ski hero owner) is a fun and typical place to eat in a 200-year-old barn near the base of the Aiguille du Midi lift. Its wonderful ambience comes with high prices.

Chamonix has great pâtisseries. The best place for a coffee, pastry, and view all at the same time is **Pâtisserie des Arcades** at 17 rue du Dr. Paccard.

Picnic assembly: A good boulangerie and a vegetable market are adjacent to the TI. The best market is the Codec, below Hôtel Alpina. There's also a supermarket on rue Vallot. The park next to the church is picnic pretty.

ALPS ADMIRATION DAY

Take today to plug your tired tourist batteries directly into the Alps. Recharge. There's not a museum or important building in sight. It's just you and Madame Nature for this vacation from your go-go vacation. If the weather's right, ride Europe's highest mountain lift to 12,600 feet.

Suggested Schedule

7:30	In line at the Aiguille du Midi lift station. After enjoying the summit, go halfway down to Plan de l'Aiguille. Walk from there to Montavernets (Mer de Glacé) and back to Chamonix.

Mountain Viewing Highlights

Alps appreciation is your goal, and Chamonix provides endless opportunities. You can get sky-high in the Alps without climbing one step, hike forever on exciting trails, or enjoy more tranquil valley floor strolls along the Arve River.

▲▲▲**Aiguille du Midi**—This is easily the valley's (and Europe's) most spectacular and popular lift. If the weather's clear, the price doesn't matter. Pile into the téléphérique and fly to the tip of a rock needle 12,600 feet above sea level. Chamonix shrinks as trees fly by, soon replaced by whizzing rocks, ice, and snow until you reach the top. No matter how sunny it is, it's cold. The air is thin. People are giddy. Fun things can happen at Aiguille du Midi if you're not too winded to join the locals in the halfway-to-heaven tango.

From the top of the lift, ride the elevator through the rock to the summit of this pinnacle. The Alps spread before you. In the distance is the bent little Matterhorn, and looming just over there is Mont Blanc, at 15,781 feet Europe's highest point.

Next, for your own private glacial dream world, get into the little red gondola and head south to Helbronner

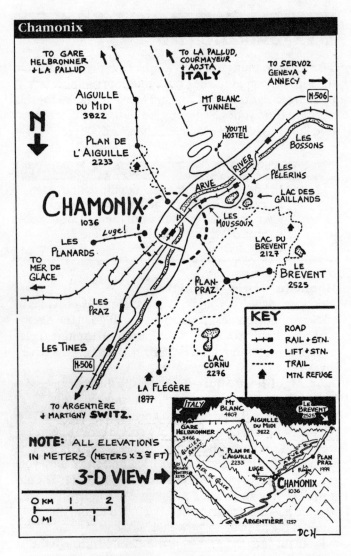

Chamonix

TO GARE HELBRONNER + LA PALLUD

TO LA PALLUD, COURMAYEUR & AOSTA **ITALY**

TO SERVOZ GENEVA & ANNECY →

N

AIGUILLE DU MIDI 3822

MT BLANC TUNNEL

N-506

YOUTH HOSTEL

LES BOSSONS

PLAN DE L'AIGUILLE 2233

RIVER

LES PELERINS

CHAMONIX 1036

ARVE

LAC DES GAILLANDS

Luge!

LES MOUSSOUX

LES PLANARDS

TO MER DE GLACE

LAC DU BREVENT 2127

LE BREVENT 2525

PLAN-PRAZ

LES PRAZ

LES TINES

N-506

LA FLÉGÈRE 1877

LAC CORNU 2276

KEY
ROAD
RAIL + STN.
LIFT + STN.
TRAIL
MTN. REFUGE

TO ARGENTIÈRE & MARTIGNY **SWITZ.**

NOTE: ALL ELEVATIONS IN METERS (METERS × 3 ≅ FT)

3-D VIEW →

0 KM 1 2
0 MI 1

ITALY

MT BLANC 4807

AIGUILLE DU MIDI 3822

LE BREVENT 2525

GARE HELBRONNER 3466

PLAN DE L'AIGUILLE 2233

PLAN PRAZ 1999

GLACIER DU GEANT

LES GRANDS MONTETS 3295

LUGE

MER DE GLACE

CHAMONIX 1036

ARGENTIÈRE 1257

—DCH—

Point, the Italian border station. It's just you and your partner, dangling silently for 40 minutes as you glide over the glacier to Italy. Hang your head out the window; explore every corner of your view. You're sailing a new sea. You can continue into Italy (see the option below), but there's really no point unless you're traveling that way.

From Aiguille du Midi, you can ride all the way back to Chamonix or just ride halfway down and hike from 7,500 feet to the valley floor at 3,400 feet. Get out at Plan de l'Aiguille (the up-and-halfway-down ticket saves you 20F) and frolic in the nearby snowfields before hiking the easy two hours to Montavernets (the Mer de Glacé). From there you can hike or ride the train back into Chamonix. Watch out for hang gliders.

To beat the clouds and crowds, ride the lifts as early as you can (up and down). To beat the major delays in August, leave by 7:00. If the weather's good, don't dilly or dally. The lift runs from 6:00-17:00 in summer, 8:00 to 16:45 in May, June, and September, and 8:00-15:45 in winter, with the last one to Helbronner at around 14:00. Approximate ticket costs: Chamonix to Plan de l'Aiguille—60F round-trip, 47F one-way; to Aiguille du Midi—140F round-trip, 106F one-way (not including parachute); all the way to Helbronner—210F round-trip, 153F one-way. It's about 20,000 lire to drop down into Italy. The youth hostel near the base gives 25 percent discount coupons to members. The elevator to the tiptop is another 12F round-trip. Avoiding that expense is a kind of Alpus-Interruptus I'd rather not experience. For a real Chamonix scene, be at the lift at 6:00 to see the colorful climbers trying to get an early start on their peak.

▲**Mer de Glacé**—A two-car cogwheel train toots you up to a rapidly moving and very dirty glacier called the Mer de Glacé, or "Sea of Ice." The glacier is interesting, as are its funky ice caves, and the views are glorious. But if you've ever seen a glacier, skip it. One good option is to go one-way and take the easy two-hour hike to the Plan de l'Aiguille, catching the lift or continuing to hike down from there. (48F round-trip, 36F one-way.)

▲**Luge**—Here's something new for the thrill-seeker in you. You can ride a chair lift up and scream down the mountain's windy, banked concrete slalom course on a wheeled sled. Chamonix has two roughly parallel luge courses, one fast and one less fast, near the Mer de Glacé. Young or old, hare or tortoise, any fit person can manage a luge. But be careful, the course is fast and slippery.

Tickets are sold one, five, or ten at a time. (25F per ride.)
   ▲▲▲ **The Téléphérique to le Brevent**—While the lift
rides aren't as spectacular on this side of the valley, the
hiking is much better and you get tremendous views of
the Mont Blanc range to the east and the Aiguilles Rouges
peaks to the west.
   Ride the *télécabine* to Planpraz (good views and hiking,
45F round-trip, 38F one-way) then catch the téléphérique up to Brevent (great views and hikes, 65F round-
trip, 46F one-way from Chamonix. Open 8:00-17:00,
closes early in off-season).
   A good hike from the Gare Brevent is Lac de l'Aiguillette
(return via Merlet), (steep but not difficult), or along the
Grand Balcon Sud to the Flegère téléphérique above Les
Praz (with a 2.5-kilometer bus ride or valley trail walk
back to Chamonix). Wherever you hike, review your
plans at the Office de Haute Montagne, bring raingear,
warm clothes, water, sunglasses, good shoes, picnic food,
and a bib for drooling at what you'll see.
   ▲ **Other Hikes**—Starting in Chamonix, the best walk is
toward Merlet along the Petit Balcon Sud. The best views
are up in Merlet. For a pleasant valley stroll, follow the
sleepy Arve River toward Les Praz (the path starts across
from the Alpina Hotel).
   For an easy and possibly the most spectacular high
country hike, ride the lift from Les Praz to La Flegère and
hike (2 easy hours each way) to Lac Blanc enjoying great
views of the Mont Blanc range. Buses leave regularly from
the TI to Les Praz. You can combine this hike with the
Grand Balcon Sud hike (and leave from Chamonix).

Itinerary Options
A Day in French-speaking Switzerland: There are
plenty of tempting alpine and cultural thrills just an hour
or two away in Switzerland. A road and a train line sneak
you scenically from Chamonix to the Swiss town of Martigny. From there, Lake Geneva, evocative Château Chil-
lon, medieval Murten, the Swiss chocolate factory tour at
Broc, the lovely capital city of Bern, and the heart of the
Swiss Alps south of Interlaken will tempt you. For more

information, see *2 to 22 Days in Germany, Austria, and Switzerland* (Santa Fe, N.M.: John Muir Publications, 1992). Remember, while train travelers cross without formalities, drivers are charged the $25 Swiss annual highway tax just to cross the border.

A Little Italy? The remote Valle d'Aosta and its historic capital city of Aosta are a short drive east of Chamonix through the Mont Blanc tunnel or a spectacular gondola ride over the Mont Blanc range. The side trip is worthwhile if you'd like to taste Italy (spaghetti, gelati, and cap

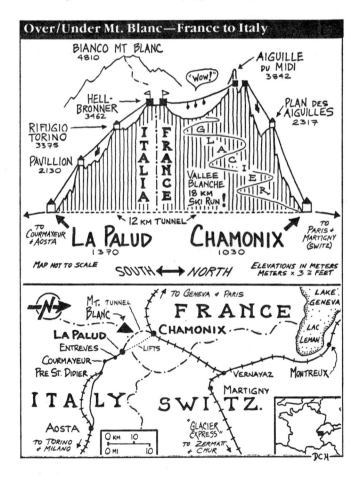

puccino), enjoy the town's great evening ambience, or
look at the ruins of Aosta, often called the "Rome of the
North." From Helbronner catch the 20,000-lire lift down
to Entreves and get to Aosta as directly as you can. To
avoid waiting for the bus, try to befriend a fellow cable
car passenger who parked at the base of the lift and hitch
a ride down the valley. Otherwise, hourly buses connect
you to Aosta (2 hours with a change in Courmeyeur). In
Aosta, sleep at **Hôtel di Rosini Renato and Maria
Rosini**. It's friendly and clean, and it has a view (inexpensive, via d'Avisa 4, 11100 Aosta, tel. from France
19-34-165-44286). The popular **Ulisse Restaurant** has
great pizza and better prices (via Ed. Aubert 58). Sit outside and watch the city cruise without cars. (If this is your
first time in Italy, their "footprint" toilet may also be a
first.) You'll notice that on the south side of the Alps your
travel dollars become like the Italian cheese—they stretch
farther. From Aosta, the train will take you to Milan and
the rest of Italy. Or the tunnel will zip you through the
dark back to Chamonix.

FROM CHAMONIX TO CHARDONNAY

Moving from France's grandest peaks to its greatest wines, you trade peaks for pinots and cable cars for chardonnays. Slalom from 5,000 feet to sea level, bypassing the diplomatic sterility of Geneva in favor of the enchanting hamlet of Brancion. Tonight's home is Burgundy's wine capital, Beaune.

Suggested Schedule

By Car:

9:00   Leave Chamonix (or, if you were rained out yesterday and it's sunny today, ride the early lift up the Aiguille du Midi).

12:30   Lunch stop in Brancion. Enjoy the welcome-to-Burgundy view.

14:00   On to Beaune, with a brief stop at Chapaize's Romanesque church.

16:00   Arrive in Beaune, check into hotel.

20:00   Burgundian feast at a hilltop restaurant overlooking Beaune.

By Train:

7:00   Leave Chamonix for Beaune (8.5 hr.). Change trains in St. Gervais (or Aix-les-Bains) and Lyon.

Driving: Chamonix to Brancion (3.5 hr.) to Beaune (1.5 hr.)

Leave Chamonix the way you came and follow the autoroute toward Geneva to Bourg-en-Bresse and Tournus. Exit the autoroute at Tournus (buy your picnic here), then follow signs to Taize and Brancion. Brancion is at the crest of a hill and needs a sign to direct you off the D-14. Be on the lookout for a tiny hill town to the right.

To reach Chapaize and Beaune, continue down the D-14. Chapaize is a short hop from Brancion. From Chapaize, follow signs to Bissey, Buxy, Chagny, and finally Beaune. In Beaune, follow the ring road around and take a right on rue du Faubourg Madeleine (just past the Calvet winery). Park in the place Madeleine.

Burgundy

Burgundy has what the rest of France wants: superior wine and cuisine, lovely countryside, and quick access east to the Alps and south to Provence. Only a small part of Burgundy's land is covered by vineyards, but winemaking is what they do best here. They've practiced since Roman times. Many will be surprised to find that the area is not named after the wine but after a fifth-century barbarian tribe, the Burgundians. Latter-day Burgundians turned Joan of Arc over to the English. Present-day Burgundians would rather talk about wine. The white cows you see everywhere are Charolais. They make France's best beef and end up in boeuf bourguignonne.

Burgundy Sightseeing Highlights

▲▲Brancion (pronounced "Bran-see-own")—This nine-building hamlet offers the purest example of Romanesque architecture I've seen—a twelfth-century church with faint frescoes inside—as well as a cute château, a fifteenth-century market hall, and a panoramic view of Burgundy. The benches in front of the church are picnic-perfect (though officially off-limits to picnickers), and the Auberge du Vieux Brancion serves a great introduction to Burgundian cuisine (expensive, but a good value). For a wonderfully peaceful break, spend a night in one of the auberge's cozy, inexpensive rooms; if you do, François's family will treat you right (tel. 85-51-03-83). If you're really on vacation and can spend the time, a night here is a must.

▲Chapaize (pronounced "Shop-ezz")—This church is famous for its eleventh-century belfry (which looks about to crumble) and its listing interior. Wander around the back for a great view of the belfry. Contrast it with the simplicity of Brancion's church. These two churches and many more that you'll see in the area owe their existence and architectural design to the nearby, once-powerful Cluny Abbey.

Itinerary Options
Annecy: This city knows how to be popular (and is ter-
ribly crowded in summer). There's something for everyone here—mountain views, a cobbled old town, canals,
flowers everywhere, a château, and a beautiful lake.
Annecy (pronounced "Ann-a-see") is France's classy Alps
city. You may not have the mountains in your lap as in
nearby Chamonix, but the distant peaks make a beautiful
picture with Annecy's lakefront setting.

If you make some time in your trip for Annecy, spend it
ambling along the canals and arcaded streets of the
delightful old city. Wander by the Palais de l'Île and under
Annecy's famous arcaded overhangs. The views are
reward enough for the hike up to the château (great picnics, skip the museum). A fine outdoor market rages on
Tuesday, Friday, and Sunday between the château and the
canal on place Ste. Claire.

Cluny and Taize: An hour and a half south of Beaune
lies the historic town of Cluny. The center of a rich and
powerful monastic movement in the Middle Ages is today
a pleasant town with very sparse and crumbled remains
of its once powerful abbey. For a new trend in monasticism,
consider visiting the booming Christian community of
Taize (pronounced "Teh-zay") just north of Cluny (pronounced "Cloo-nee"). Brother Roger and his community
welcome visitors who'd like to spend a few days getting
close to God through meditation, singing, and simple living. Call or write first if you plan to stay overnight. (The
cost is 25F for a dorm bed. Write to: Taize Community,
71250 Cluny; tel. 85-50-14-14.)

Beaune
You'll feel comfortable right away in this hardworking
but fun-loving capital of the world's most serious wine
region. Beaune is a compact, thriving little city with vineyards on its doorstep. Life here centers around the
production and consumption of the prestigious, expensive Côte d'Or wines. Côte d'Or means "golden hillsides,"
a spectacle to enjoy in late October as the leaves of the
vineyards turn.

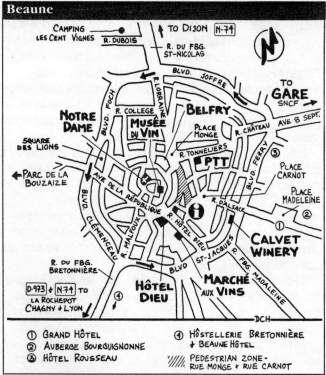

Limit your Beaune (pronounced "Bone") ramblings to the town center, contained within its medieval walls and circled by a one-way ring road. All roads and activities seem to converge on the quintessentially French place Carnot. The TI, across the street from the Hôtel Dieu (Hospice de Beaune) on the place de la Halle (from place Carnot, walk toward the thin spire), has city maps, brochures on Beaune hotels and restaurants, a roomfinding service, CH pamphlets, and advice on winery tours and tastings, concerts, and events. (Open April to October 9:00-20:00; otherwise 9:00-19:00, tel. 80-22-24-51.) Half-day tasting tour minibuses leave from the TI twice a day (160F).

Beaune has a rare wine-soaked charm. Its tourist office gives Americans a free bottle of Burgundy on the 4th of July.

Accommodations

Hôtel Le Home, Beaune's best two-star hotel value, is a half-mile out of town on the N-74 toward Dijon (moderate, on your right at 38 route de Dijon, call ahead—it's popular, tel. 80-22-16-43).

Auberge Bourguignonne is petit, clean, and comfortable (moderate, on place Madeleine, tel. 80-22-23-53) but they require you to eat dinner there and are less than friendly.

Hôtel au Grand St. Jean is the biggest hotel in town with 106 rooms and variable bed quality. Color blind travelers will love their TV lounge (moderate, on place Madeleine, tel. 80-24-12-22). English spoken by Claude Neaux and his father, Claude Neaux (pronounced "no").

Hôtel Rousseau is ideal for those really traveling on the cheap, with cheap, basic rooms, pet birds everywhere, and no showers at all (cheap, at 11 place Madeleine, tel. 80-22-13-59).

Driving into Beaune, you'll pass two excellent hotels before reaching the city center. The ugly **Beaune Hôtel** (moderate, 55 Faubourg Bretonnière, tel. 80-22-11-01) and the better **Hostellerie Bretonnière** (moderate, 43 Faubourg Bretonnière, tel. 80-22-15-77) are convenient if you're traveling by car but a good 10 minutes by foot from the city center.

Train travelers will appreciate the conventional, reasonable, **Hôtel de France**, right across from the station (moderate, 35 avenue du 8 Septembre, tel. 80-24-10-34).

Chambres d'Hôte: The Côte d'Or has great CHs. Most can be found only in small wine villages, and many are only a short drive from Beaune. One I particularly like is in Magny-les-Villers. From Beaune, go north on the N-74, then west at Ladoix. The **Dumays** have two attached rooms with private shower and W.C. in a restored farmhouse, great for three or more (inexpensive, located behind the church, tel. 80-62-91-16). The **Paulet family** in Baubigny offers fine rooms, a huge yard and a peaceful setting just below La Rochepot castle (21340 Nolay, tel. 85-47-32-18).

CAMPGROUND

One of France's best campgrounds, **Les Cent Vignes**, is a short walk from the town center. This place is fully equipped with a great restaurant, bar, and small store (10 rue Auguste-Dubois, follow signs toward Dijon and look for camping signs, tel. 80-22-03-91).

Burgundy Cuisine and Wine

Your taste buds are going to thank you for bringing them here. Considered by many to be France's best, Burgundian cuisine is peasant cooking elevated to an art. Burgundy is home to several classic dishes such as *escargots bourguignonne* (snails served sizzling hot in garlic butter), *boeuf bourguignonne* (beef simmered for hours in red wine with onions and mushrooms), coq au vin (chicken stewed in red wine), and the famous Dijon mustards. Look also for *jambon persillé* (cold ham layered in a garlic-parsley gelatin), *pain d'épices* (spice bread), and *gougère* (light, puffy cheese pastries). Native cheeses are Epoisses and Langres (both mushy and great) and my favorite, Montrachet (a tasty goat cheese). Crème de Cassis (a black currant liqueur) is another Burgundian specialty; you'll find it in desserts and snazzy drinks (try a kir).

Along with Bordeaux, Burgundy is why France is famous for wine. You'll find it all here—great reds, whites, and rosés. The key grapes are Chardonnay (producing dry, white wines) and Pinot Noir (producing medium-bodied red wines). Every village produces its own distinctive wine (usually named after the village— like Chablis and Meursault). Look for the Dégustation Gratuite (free tasting) signs and prepare for serious tasting and steep prices if you buy. The least expensive (but still excellent) wines are the Bourgogne Aligote (white), Bourgogne ordinaire and Passetoutgrain (both red), and those from the Macon, Chalon, and Beaujolais areas. If you like rosé, try the Marsannay, considered the best rosé in France.

A good budget place to eat is **Camping les Cents Vignes**, where you'll find some of the best escargots in town. If it's a nice evening, you feel like a 15-minute walk and you've never seen a European campground, try it! You'll find a pleasant terrace or indoor tables, a friendly crowd, and a good menu at reasonable prices. Take a stroll through the campground and notice where the cars are from (inexpensive; 10 rue Dubois, in the direction of Dijon; restaurant open April to September).

Central Beaune's best budget restaurant is the **Relais de la Madeleine** at 44 place Madeleine (especially good lamb chops and fresh trout), tel. 80-22-07-47. The **Picboeuf** is another good bet for dinner (75 yards from place Madeleine where rue d'Alsace meets the ring road).

For fine dining near Beaune, try **Le Relais de la Diligence**. Come here to surround yourself with vineyards and taste the area's best budget Burgundian cuisine with many menu options (inexpensive/moderate; take the N-74 toward Chagny and make a left at L'Hôpital Meursault on the D-23; closed Tuesday evenings and Wednesday; tel. 80-21-21-32). **Au Bon Accueil** is my favorite; on a hill overlooking Beaune (Montagne de Beaune), it has the friendliest Portuguese waitress I've met in France. Try the coq au vin. (Moderate; to get there, leave Beaune's ring road and take the Bligny sur Ouche turnoff. A few minutes outside Beaune, you'll see signs to the Sans Souci Disco and Au Bon Accueil; tel. 80-22-08-80, closed Wednesday.)

For picnics, go to the charcuterie on rue Monge and pick up a slice of the jambon persillé (pronounced "zham-bone pehrsill-ay"). Get your cheese at **Taste Frommage**, across the street on rue Carnot. How about that for a French stench? Gather the rest of your needs at any épicerie. There's a Casino supermarket just off place Madeleine, through the archway.

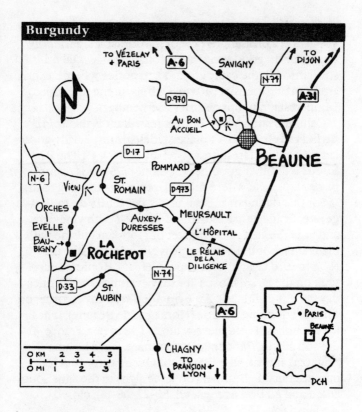

Burgundy

A TASTE OF BURGUNDY

Today it's Burgundy's best—from Beaune's one-of-a-kind medieval hospital to the area's top castle through beautiful countryside to sample of some of the world's best wines. The grand finale is dinner in a restaurant surrounded by a vineyard.

Suggested Schedule

By Car:

9:00	Tour the Hôtel Dieu (hospital).
10:30	See the Basilique Collégiale Notre Dame.
11:15	Wander the pedestrian streets. Assemble your picnic.
12:45	Head for La Rochepot.
13:15	Picnic with great view of the château at La Rochepot.
14:30	Tour La Rochepot Château.
15:30	Scenic ride back to Beaune via the site of the world's biggest and best hidden wine press.
17:00	Wine smorgasbord at Beaune's Marché aux Vins.
20:00	Dinner in the foothills.

By Foot and Bike:

9:00	Tour Hôtel Dieu.
10:30	See the Basilique Collégiale Notre Dame and enjoy Beaune.
12:30	Rent a bike and pedal through the vineyards.
17:00	Wine smorgasbord at the Marché aux Vins.
20:00	Dinner at Beaune's campground.

Driving: Beaune to La Rochepot to Beaune
Get on the ring road and take the Nolay-Meursault turn-off, then follow the D-973 to La Rochepot. In La Rochepot, look hard for the left turn toward St. Aubin (D-33). A dreamy picnic pullout is 100 yards up the road.

   La Rochepot to Beaune via Scenic Route: Drive over the hill from the château and follow the signs to Baubigny, then Evelle. In Evelle, find the Auberge du Vieux Pressoir (faded sign) and walk down the steps

across the street to discover a gargantuan wine press.
Leave Evelle going to Orches. Stop at the view point.
That's St. Romain straight down. Continue on to the D-17
and follow it back into Beaune via Pommard.

Bus Routes

Transco buses run fixed route schedules from Beaune
through the Côte d'Or but strand you in La Rochepot for
five hours. Minibus wine tasting tours (five times daily
from the TI for about 160F) will get you through the
countryside and to wineries you couldn't get into otherwise. See the TI for information on both.

Bike Route

Rent a bike at the station. The ride to La Rochepot (see
driving route) is a grueling uphill pedal, but possible. It's
downhill all the way back (well, almost). Consider the
long (all day), scenic route via the D-33 to St. Aubin, then
find the tiny road from Gamay to Puligny, Montrachet,
and Meursault. To give your legs a break, ride instead
along the D-18 to Savigny-les-Beaune and Pernand Verge-
lesses. (Check out Savigny's unusual château.)

Sightseeing Hightlights

▲▲▲ **Hôtel Dieu**—The Hundred Years War and Black
Death devastated Beaune, leaving over 90 percent of its
population destitute. Nicholas Rolin, Chancellor of Burgundy and a peasant by birth, had to do something for
"his people." So, in 1443, he paid to build this flamboyant
Flemish-Gothic charity hospital. It was completed in
only eight years. Tour it on your own; you'll find (for
once) good English explanations (pick up description at
ticket desk). How about those medical instruments?
Yeow! The pharmacy once provided slug-slime cures for
sore throats and cockroach powders for constipation.
Next, shuffle into a dark room to admire Van der Wey-
den's dramatic *The Last Judgment* polyptych, commis-
sioned by Rolin to give the dying something to ponder.
Your visit ends after the magnifying glass demonstration
(ask the guard to do it) with a look at Flemish tapestries.
The Story of Jacob, woven by one person in 17 years, is
magnificent. (Admission 24F, open 9:00-18:30 Easter

through November, otherwise 9:00-11:40 and 14:00-18:00.)
▲**Basilique Collégiale Notre Dame**—Built in the
twelfth and thirteenth centuries, this is a good example of
Cluny-style architecture. Enter to see the fifteenth-
century tapestries (behind the altar, drop in a franc for
lights), a variety of stained glass, and what's left of frescoes depicting the life of Lazarus. (Open 9:00-12:00 and
14:00-18:00.) Next door is the free, interesting courtyard
of the Musée du Vin.

Musée du Vin—You don't have to like wine to appreciate this folk-wine museum. The history and culture of
Burgundy and wine were fermented in the same bottle.
Wander into the courtyard for a look at the Duke's Palace
and antique wine presses. Inside the museum you'll find
tools, costumes, and scenes of Burgundian wine history
but no tasting. There's a fine model of the wine region;
light up St. Romain, Auxey Duress, and Meursault, this
afternoon's route. Can you find the naked grape stomp-
ers? If you ever wondered how the wine bottle got its
shape, you'll enjoy the last room. (Admission 11F, ticket
good for other Beaune museums. Open April to September 9:00-11:30 and 13:30-18:30; otherwise, 10:00-11:30
and 14:00-17:00.)

▲▲▲**Marché aux Vins (Wine Market)**—This is Burgundy's wine smorgasbord and the best way to sample
(and buy) its awesome array of wines. You pay 40F plus
10F for a tasting cup (refundable, but why not keep it as a
souvenir), get a *tastevin* (official tasting cup) and 45
minutes (though I've spent an hour and a half here) to sip
away at Burgundy's beloved. Plunge into the labyrinth of
candlelit caves dotted with 39 wine-barrel tables, each
home to a new bottle of wine to taste. You're on your
own. Take your time. This is world-class stuff. The $80
reds come upstairs in the old chapel at the end. (Hint:
taste better and longer by sneaking in some bread or
crackers.) If you grab a wine carton at the beginning and
at least pretend you're going to buy some bottles, the
occasional time checker will leave you alone. (Open
9:00-12:00, 14:00-18:30, last entry 18:00.)

While the Marché aux Vins is the ultimate wine-tasting
experience, Beaune has many wineries that show visitors

around and give samples. The TI has specifics. Wine
lovers should visit the impressive Atheneum book/wine
shop across the street.

Parc de la Bouzaise—This pleasant zoo to come to and
relax, do some people-watching, and sleep off the wine
is just outside the city walls on avenue de la République.

Near Beaune

▲▲Château La Rochepot—This is a great mom and
pop castle. The sign across the drawbridge asks you to
knock three times with the ancient knocker, then push
the doorbell. Often no one comes, so you just enter on
your own. Serge Robin or his wife will eventually greet
you and take you "srou zee castle" (he learned his English
at age 65). Be ready for "zee grapplene ook" and "zee
craws-a-bow." This castle is splendid inside and out. The
kitchen will bowl you over. Look for the fifteenth-
century highchair in the dining room. Don't leave the
castle without climbing the tower and seeing the Chinese
room, singing chants in the resonant chapel, and making
ripples in the well. (Can you spit a bull's-eye? It's 72
meters down!) And don't leave the charming town of La
Rochepot without driving, walking, or pedaling up the
D-33 toward St. Aubin for a romantic view of this classi-
cally Burgundian castle. (Admission 18F, open June to
August 10:00-11:30 and 14:30-18:00; shoulder season
10:00-11:30 and 14:30-16:00; closed Tuesday and from
November to Easter. Tel. 80-21-71-37.)

**▲▲Chateauneuf en Auxois and Abbey of La
Bussiere**—For a fine circular side trip from Beaune, visit
this superbly preserved medieval hill town/castle (great
views of Burgundy canal and friendly café on the main
square). From Beaune's ring road, take the Bligny sur
Ouche turnoff. After Bligny sur Ouche, head for Pont de
Pany. At Pont d'Ouche, turn left and follow the canal. In
about ten minutes you'll see Chateauneuf's brooding,
hard-to-miss castle. After Chateauneuf, follow signs to La
Bussiere (look hard) and drive into its abbey grounds.
Wander into the abbey and ask for the keys to the church
and *pressoir*. From the abbey, go back to Pont d'Ouche,
turn left, and follow signs home to Beaune.

FROM BURGUNDY TO ALSACE

After a morning in France's spicy mustard capital, head north along the beautiful Doubs River and finish your day in Alsace, where France has a German accent.

Suggested Schedule

9:00	Train or drive to Dijon.
9:45	Walking tour of Dijon.
11:00	Tour Musée des Beaux Arts, quick lunch.
14:00	Train or drive to Colmar (train via Besançon; always verify train schedule).
17:30	Arrive in Colmar.

Driving: Beaune to Dijon (40 min.) to Colmar (3.5 hr.)
The N-74 will get you to Dijon quickly. In Dijon, follow the signs to Centre-ville, then Syndicat d'Initiative—it gets tricky. Park as close to the TI as you can.

From Dijon to Colmar, you have several options. The fastest route is by way of Dole (signs for Geneve) and the autoroute. Except for crossing through the cities of Besançon and Belfort, the local routes are quick and scenic. I like the route that leaves Dijon in the direction of Gray. A few miles after leaving Dijon, you'll see the Besançon/Pontailler turnoff (D-70). Track the signs to Besançon via Pontailler and Marnay, being careful not to take a premature right on the D-475. In Besançon, take N-83 north to Belfort. There's a scenic, friendly café road stop just past the hamlet of Sechin (a few miles before Baume-les-Dames). The cliff-hanging chalet/bar on your right has panoramic views and outdoor tables. Continue on the N-83 to Isle-sur-Doubs, then join the autoroute and follow it to the Colmar off-ramp. In Colmar, follow signs to Centre-ville and park at the place Rapp.

Sightseeing Highlights
▲▲ **Dijon**—Beaune may be Burgundy's wine capital, but prosperous and sprawling Dijon is its undisputed economic

powerhouse and true capital. Begin at the TI (closed from 12:00-14:00 daily, except in summer, tel. 80-43-42-12). Pick up the English walking tour brochure and, using its map and description, follow this route for a full dose of Dijon's half-timbered houses, busy pedestrian streets, and beautiful churches.

Head through the arch at the other end of place Darcy. Walk straight down rue de la Liberté past the famous Grey Poupon store to place Rude. Soak up the ambience at place Rude, saunter left to the rue Musette, then turn right toward the Venetian-like facade of Notre Dame.

Dijon's **Église de Notre Dame**, gushing with gargoyles, is a fine example of thirteenth-century Burgundian design. Notice the clock Jacquemart above the right tower; for 600 years it has rung out the time in three-part harmony. Mosey into and then around Notre Dame to the antiques of rue Verrerie. At rue Chardonnerie, take a quick peek at the facade of #28, then double back on rue Verrerie to rue des Forges. Notice the facade above Les Florentines and enter the courtyard at the Syndicat d'Initiative. Spy on the bank, then climb the stairs to the midget balcony. At place Rude, walk down rue de la Liberté to the **Musée de Beaux Arts**, one of France's truly great art museums.

After leaving the museum, continue down rue de la Liberté to **Église St. Michel** at the end of the street. The church's exterior is a jumble of sixteenth-century Gothic and Renaissance styles (notice the wild detail over the doorways). The interior's reddish stone basks in the stained-glass-filtered light. Return to your starting point, taking time to admire the classic design of the place de la Liberation and the shops along rues du Bourg and Boussuet.

▲▲▲**Dijon's Musée des Beaux Arts**—This excellent museum has a little something for everyone. Besides its fine collection of European paintings from all periods, you can see the five-chimneyed kitchen (ground floor), the Salle des Gardes, home to two incredibly ornate tombs (climb the stairs to the balcony for the best angle), the sculptures of Carpeaux and Rude near the Salles des

Gardes, a 3-D modern art room, and the huge model of the once-glorious Palais des Ducs de Bourgogne—to your right as you enter the museum. (Admission 12F, good for all Dijon, museums free on Sunday. Open 10:00-18:00, closed Tuesday. Sunday 10:00-12:30 and 14:00-18:00.)

Alsace

The French province of Alsace stands like a flower-child referee between Germany and France. Bounded by the Rhine on the east and the softly rolling Vosges Mountains on the west, this is a lush land of villages, vineyards, ruined castles, and almost naive cheeriness. Wine is the primary industry, topic of conversation, dominant mouthwash, perfect excuse for countless festivals, and a tradition that provides the foundation for the rest of the Alsatian culture.

Because of its location, natural wealth, naked vulnerability, and the fact that Germany thinks the mountains are the natural border while France thinks the Rhine is, Alsace has changed hands several times, and nearly every Alsatian generation has weathered an invasion. Having been a political pawn between Germany and France for a thousand years, Alsace has a hybrid culture. This Gallic-Teutonic mix is seen in many ways. Restaurants serve sauerkraut with fine sauces behind half-timbered Bavarian gables. Most locals who swear do so bilingually, and many of the towns have German names.

Colmar

Colmar is a well-pickled old place of 70,000 offering heavyweight sights in a warm small-town package. It's the best base for exploring the nearby villages, castles, and route du vin.

Historic beauty was usually a poor excuse to be spared the ravages of World War II, but it worked for Colmar. The American and British military were careful not to bomb the half-timbered old burghers' houses, characteristic red and green tiled roofs, and cobbled lanes of Alsace's most beautiful city.

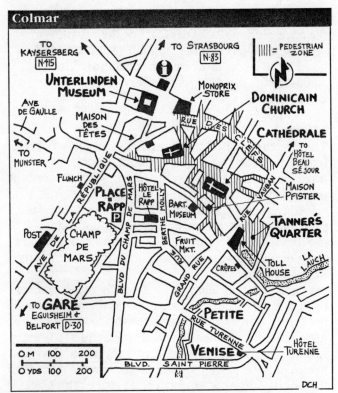

Today, Colmar thrives with historic buildings, impressive art treasures, and the popular Alsatian cuisine that attracts eager palates from all over Europe. And Colmar has that special French talent of being great but cozy at the same time. Schoolgirls park their rickety horse carriage in front of the city hall ready to give visitors a clip-clop tour of the old town. Antique shops welcome browsers, and hotel managers run down the sleepy streets to pick up fresh croissants in time for breakfast.

There isn't a straight street in Colmar. Thankfully, it's a lovely town to be lost in. Navigate by the high church steeples. The TI is next to the Unterlinden Museum. Head down rue Kleber from the corner of place Rapp, then look for signs. The TI has a board listing all the hotels, with "complet" signs posted if they're full (not always accurate). They can reserve a room in a hotel or CH for you. Pick up their city map and route du vin map and, if you lack wheels, ask for the "Colmar Actualités," a booklet with bus schedules. Ask about Colmar's Folklore Tuesdays (weekly in summer), Sauerkraut Days in late August/early September, the local wine festival in August, and other nearby wine festivals. (Open weekdays in July and August 9:00-12:30 and 13:30-19:00, Saturday 9:00-12:00 and 14:00-17:00, and Sunday 9:00-12:30. Otherwise Monday to Friday 9:00-12:00 and 14:00-18:00, Saturday 9:00-12:00. Tel. 89-41-02-29. Colmar is most crowded from June 1 through September 5. Good public W.C. 20 yards to the left of the TI.)

Accommodations

Hotels are jammed on weekends in June, September, and October. July and August are busy, but there are always rooms—somewhere. Try to stay near the city center, away from the train station.

With 40 new rooms, the **Hôtel Le Rapp** has lost much of its charm, but the owner is still Saint Bernard to me. Bernard runs this hotel-restaurant, mixing class with warmth like no other man I've met. He still has a few bargain rooms in the old section (moderate, rue Berthe-Molley, tel. 89-41-62-10). You choose—old and funky or new rooms with TVs. The alley rooms can be noisy. Unless you're in a hurry, eat here for a taste of French elegance with impeccable service.

Hôtel Beau Séjour is a decent value, with a new swimming pool. (moderate, 25 rue du Ladhof, a 10-minute walk from the center, tel. 89-41-37-16).

Hôtel Turenne caters to the business traveler, so you can't avoid a TV and full bathroom, but this is still a fine hotel in a great location (moderate/expensive, 10 route du Bale, tel. 89-41-12-26). Try for a room off the street.

Primo 99 is France's pre-fab hotel, a modern, efficient, bright, nothing-but-the-plastic-and-concrete-basics place to sleep for those to whom ambience is a four-letter word and modernity is next to godliness (inexpensive, 5 rue des Ancêtres, tel. 89-24-22-24).

The best cheap beds (in large rooms) in Colmar are at the **Maison des Jeunes** (Camille-Schlumberger 17, near the station in a comfortable and fairly central location, tel. 89-41-26-87). The desk is open from 14:00 to 23:00. The **youth hostel**, open March through October, also has very cheap dorm beds (2 rue Pasteur, a 15-minute walk from the station and downtown, tel. 89-80-57-39).

Chambres d'Hôte: Maison Jund, my favorite urban French CH, in Colmar's old city, is a magnificent half-timbered house. It's a medieval tree house soaked in wine and filled with flowers. The rooms are equipped with kitchenettes and full bathrooms but are generally available only from mid-June to mid-September (cheap, 12 rue de l'Ange, tel. 89-41-58-72). Mr. Jund offers a fun wine tasting.

For a small-town alternative, consider these private homes in nearby Eguisheim: **Mr. Hertz-Meyer**, 3 rue du Reisling, tel. 89-23-67-74; **Mr. Stoeckle Muller**, 5 rue de Bruxelles, tel. 89-23-19-50; and **Mr. Stocky Gilbert**, 24 rue de Colmar, tel. 89-41-68-04.

Alsatian Cuisine

Alsatian cuisine is a major tourist attraction itself. You can't miss the German influence. Try the *choucroute* (sauerkraut and sausage), smelly Meunster cheese, pretzels, and *backenoffe* (potato, meat, and onion stew). The native *tarte à l'oignon* (like an onion quiche, but better), fresh trout, *foie gras* (fattened goose liver), and Alsatian cheesecake will bring you back to France. Alsatian wines, while less loved than Burgundy's, are great and much cheaper. The local specialties are Riesling (drier than you're used to), Gerwurztztraminer (a spicy before-dinner wine), Sylvaner (the cheapest), Tokay, and the tasty Crémant d'Alsace (champagne). You'll also see Eaux-de-Vie, a powerful fruit-flavored brandy; try the *framboise* (raspberry) flavor.

In Colmar, the **Hôtel Restaurant Le Rapp** is my dress-up, high-cuisine splurge. I comb my hair, change my socks, and savor a slow, elegant meal served with grace and fine Alsatian wine. Bernard and Dominique won't let you or your taste buds down. (Moderate/expensive, closed Wednesday, air-conditioned.) **Au Café de Colmar** probably serves the best 75F menu in town, as well as excellent à la carte selections (located above Matelas Herzog at the intersection of rues Stanislas and Kleber, across from the Hôtel Kempf).

Au Pave d'Alsace (moderate-expensive, 14 rue Etroite, just off rue Rapp in the pedestrian zone) is owned by a very likable French couple who spent three years in the U.S.A. and miss it. Perfect English and very fine cuisine in a traditional Alsatian setting.

In the Tanners Quarter and La Petite Venise, Colmar's most scenic dining locale, you'll find several reasonable restaurants and cafés. For crêpes with atmosphere, eat at **Crêperie Tom Pouce**, located right downtown (inexpensive, 10 rue des Tanneurs). Next door, the **Restaurant des Tanneurs Weinstub** is a bit more upscale, with fine Alsatian menus from 85F. For canalfront dining, head into La Petite Venise to the bridge on rue Turenne, where you'll find a pizzeria, a weinstub café (both cheap), and a fine canal-level restaurant, **Les Bateliers** (moderate).

Two good self-services dish up low-stress meals in sterile settings. **Flunch**, on place Rapp, is more pleasant but pricier than the **Monoprix** cafeteria. The best self-service option is downstairs in the Monoprix market, where you'll find sensational lunch and dinner picnic fixin's at the fish and meat counters. Ask for a petite portion and a plastic fork and find a French bench.

If it's hot (which it normally is in summer), buy a picnic at Monoprix and cool your ankles with the locals in the fountain in the park at place Rapp.

COLMAR AND THE ROUTE DU VIN

The morning's yours to explore Colmar's old center and impressive art. Shoppers love Colmar. Your afternoon will be filled with storks and the cutest wine villages in Europe. If you've been dying to test your German, today's your big chance. Whatever you do, work up an appetite for a first-class Alsatian dinner.

Suggested Schedule

8:30	Orientation walk ending at tourist office.
9:00	Unterlinden Museum.
10:30	Free time to cruise Colmar, lunch.
13:30	Explore the wine road and villages by car or bike.
19:30	Dine Alsatian-style back in Colmar.

Driving

The easiest approach to the route du vin is to leave Colmar following signs to Strasbourg and Selestat (N-83). Exit at signs to Kaysersberg and you're in the heart of the wine route (details below). Michelin's yellow regional map is very helpful.

Train/Bus/Bike

Public buses connect Colmar with most route du vin villages (details below). The schedules are fairly convenient, particularly to Kaysersberg and Riquewihr. Ask at the TI for the "Actualités Colmar" schedule. More than one company often provides service to the same town, so check all the schedules.

Trains between Colmar and Strasbourg are frequent and take only 30 minutes.

You can rent a bike at the station (tel. 89-23-17-17) or at the Peugeot bike store next to the Unterlinden Museum. Kaysersberg and Eguisheim, just three or four miles apart, are fine biking destinations.

Sightseeing Highlights

▲▲▲ **Unterlinden Museum**—Colmar's touristic claim to fame, this is one of my favorite museums in Europe. Its extensive, yet manageable, collection ranges from Roman Colmar to medieval winemaking exhibits to traditional wedding dresses to babies' cribs to Picasso.

The highlight of the museum (and, for me, the city) is Grünewald's gripping Isenheim Altarpiece, actually a series of paintings on hinges that pivot like shutters (study the little model on the wall). Designed to help people in a hospital endure horrible skin diseases long before the age of painkillers, it's one of the most powerful paintings ever produced. Stand petrified in front of it and let the agony and suffering of the Crucifixion drag its gnarled fingers down your face. Just as you're about to break down and sob with those in the painting, turn to the happy ending—a psychedelic explosion of resurrection joy. It's like jumping from the dentist's chair directly into a Jacuzzi. For a reminder that the Middle Ages didn't have a monopoly on grief, stop at the museum's full-sized cloth copy of Picasso's *Guernica*. (Admission 25F. Open 9:00-18:00 daily, closed Tuesday in off-season.)

▲▲ **Dominican Church**—Here is another medieval mindblower. In Colmar's Église des Dominicains, you'll find Martin Schongauer's angelically beautiful *Virgin of the Rosebush*, which looks like it was painted yesterday, holding court on center stage. (Admission 8F. Open 10:00-18:00 daily.)

Tanners' Quarters—This refurbished chunk of the old town is a delight, day or night. There is outdoor wine tasting here many summer evenings.

Bartholdi Museum—This interesting little museum recalls the life and work of the local boy who gained fame by sculpting the Statue of Liberty. Several of his statues, usually with one arm raised high, grace Colmar's squares. (Open April-October 10:00-12:00 and 14:00-18:00. Off-season on weekends only, at 30 rue des Marchands.)

▲▲ **Route du Vin**—Alsace's wine road, the route du vin, is an asphalt ribbon tying ninety miles of vineyards, vil-

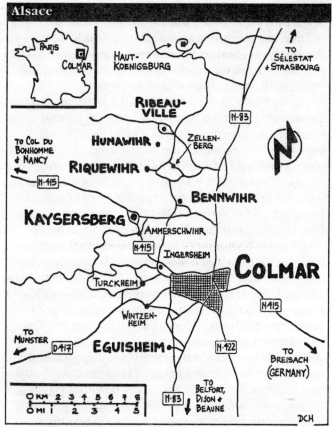

Alsace

lages, and feudal fortresses into an understandably popular tourist package. The dry, sunny climate makes for
good wine and happy tourists. It's been a wine center
since Roman days. As you drive through 30,000 acres of
vineyards blanketing the hills from Marlenheim to Thann,
you'll see how vinocentric this area is.

If you have only one afternoon, limit yourself to these
towns:

Eguisheim—Just a few miles (a flat and easy bike ride)
from Colmar, this scenic little town is best explored by
walking around its circular road, then cutting through the
middle. Visit the Eguisheim Wine Cooperative. (Cave
vinicole d'Eguisheim, 6 Grand Rue, tel. 89-22-20-20;

folklore and tastings summer Wednesdays 17:00-19:00; open 10:00-11:00 and 14:00-17:00.)

Kaysersberg—Albert Schweitzer's hometown is larger but just as cute as Eguisheim. Climb to the castle, browse through the art galleries, enjoy the colorful bundle of fifteenth-century houses near the fortified town bridge, visit Dr. Schweitzer's house, check out the church with its impressive 400-year-old altarpiece, taste some wine, and wander along nearby vineyards. (Kaysersberg TI, tel. 89-78-22-78.)

Riquewihr—Very cute and very commercial, this little walled village is filled with shops, cafés, art galleries, cobblestone streets, and flowers. Tasting and tours can be found at Caves Dopff et Irion, Cour du Château, tel. 89-47-92-51. (TI tel. 89-47-80-80.)

Hunawhir—Another bit of wine-soaked Alsatian cuteness complete with an interesting fortified church and great views.

Dégustation along Alsace's Wine Road—Throughout Alsace you'll see Dégustation signs. Dégustation means "come on in and taste," and *gratuit* means "free"; otherwise, there's a small charge. Most towns have wineries that give tours. Eguisheim's and Riquewihr's are good. Bennwihr's modern cooperative, created after the destruction during World War II, provides a fascinating look at a more modern and efficient method of production. Your hotel receptionist or the people at the TI can give you advice or even telephone a winery for you to confirm tour times. You may have to wait for a group and tag along for a tour and free tasting. Be sure to try Crémant, the Alsatian "champagne." It's very good—and much cheaper. The French words for headache, if you really get "Alsaced," are *mal à la tete.*

Storks—There's a must-see stork living in a fourteenth-century tower in Ribeauville, and if you like that, there's a whole stork park in nearby Hunawhir (Fee 12F, 24F to see the afternoon spectacle, park opens at 14:00).

▲**Strasbourg Cathedral**—This uniquely Alsatian cathedral, with its tall, slender spire and multicolored tile and red stone roof is well worth a side trip. Approach the cathedral on foot from place Gutenberg and rue Mercière. It's particularly stunning in the late afternoon light. Don't miss the doomsday pillar and fifteenth-century astronomical clock inside or the walk up the tower (8F, open 9:00-18:00); the view is worth the struggle. Afterward, take a stroll through Strasbourg's enchanting La Petite France—follow signs from place Gutenberg. Strasbourg, a large city, is an easy side trip from Colmar or a stop en route to Paris.

Helpful Hints

Colmar is a good place for mailing things if your parcel is under ten pounds. (Posting in Paris can be a headache.) The post office near place Rapp, with its postboxes for sale and postal clerks as cheery, speedy, and multilingual as yours at home, is a good place to lighten your load (open 8:00-19:00). Colmar is also a good place to do laundry (self-service laundromats are at rue Turenne near Petite Venise and 1 rue Ruest, just off the pedestrian street rue Vauban, normally open daily 8:00-21:00) and to shop (many stores close Monday mornings).

THE LONG HAUL BACK TO PARIS, STOPPING AT VERDUN AND REIMS

Today you complete this 22-day circle, traveling all the way across France to Paris with a stop to remember World War I at Verdun and an afternoon at the Gothic cathedral in Reims. You'll be back in Paris in time for dinner and a farewell evening stroll.

Suggested Schedule

By Car:

7:00	Leave Colmar. Breakfast at rest stop en route.
11:00	See the battlefields and monuments of Verdun. Lunch.
13:30	Continue to Reims.
14:45	See the cathedral at Reims.
16:00	Take the autoroute back to Paris, turn in rental car.
19:00	Romantic last night dinner in your favorite Parisian neighborhood.

By Train:

7:07	Train to Strasbourg (40 min.).
8:00	Train from Strasbourg to Epernay (3.25 hr.).
12:16	Train from Epernay to Reims (20 min.).
13:00	Visit Reims Cathedral and maybe tour a champagne cave.
16:06	Train from Reims to Paris (1.5 hr.).
20:30	Romantic last night dinner in your favorite Parisian neighborhood.

Note: There's a night train option leaving Colmar at 21:51 and arriving in Paris at 6:48 the next morning (transfer in Strasbourg).

Driving: Colmar to Verdun (4 hr.) to Reims (1 hr.) to Paris (1.5 hr.)

Leave Colmar on the N-83 toward Strasbourg, which becomes the autoroute (A-4). Verdun is about a half hour after Metz on the autoroute. Take the Verdun off-ramp and head into the city if you need food. Otherwise, pass

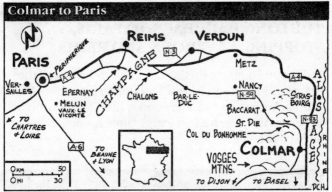

Colmar to Paris

through the city onto the N-3 toward Etain, following signs to Champs de Bataille, Rive Droite. (The battlefield remains are situated on two sides of the Meuse River; the Rive Droite is the more interesting.) Follow signs to Fort Douamant. (From October to March, Verdun sights close from 12:00 to 14:00, so those driving from Colmar will have to hustle.)

From Verdun, return to the autoroute to Paris, passing lots of strange, goofy, modern Franco-freeway art. Take the Reims exit marked "Cathédrale," and you'll see your destination. Park near the church. (If you skip Verdun, the park next to the church's entrance is great for picnics— public W.C., dangerous grass, glorious setting.)

Back on the freeway, it's a straight shot (except for toll-booths) into Paris. (Remember, if you're renting a car, you could turn it in on arrival in Colmar and ride the night train into Paris.)

By Train

There are good connections from Colmar to Reims and from Reims to Paris (5 hours total). Or consider the over-night train option to Paris via Strasbourg. The scenery between Colmar and Paris is rather dull, and Chartres Cathedral near Paris is as good as Reims, so you're not missing much—well, except a night in a hotel. This also gives you an extra day in Alsace and plenty of time to explore Strasbourg. Verdun requires a car. Another way to

streamline is to skip the Reims stop and do the champagne tour in Epernay, a stop on the Colmar-Paris train.

Verdun
Little remains in Europe today to remind us of World War
I. Verdun provides a fine tribute to the over one million
lives lost in the World War I battles here. Forests have
overgrown the trench-filled battlefields that surround the
city of Verdun. You could spend several days exploring
the battlefield monuments, but in two hours you can see
the most impressive ones and appreciate the awesome
scale of the battles. Start with the Memorial-Musée de
Fleury, where you'll see reconstructed scenes and models
of the battles that raged for over four years. (Fee 18F,
open mid-March to mid-September 9:00-18:00; off-
season 9:00-12:00 and 14:00-17:30.) Consider a visit to
Fort Douaumont (a bit farther down the road) to tour an

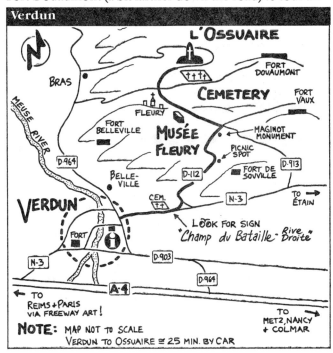

underground fort, a bunker, and tunnels and see the
remains of a World War I command control center.

   Don't miss the tomb of the 130,000 French and Germans,
whose last home was the muddy trenches of Verdun, at
the strange monument of L'Ossuaire de Douaumont
(same hours as the museum). Look through the low windows for a gloomy memorial to those whose political and
military leaders asked them to make the "ultimate sacrifice" for their countries. Enter the monument and experience a humbling and moving tribute. Ponder a war that
left half of all the men in France between ages 15 and 30
dead or wounded. See the 20-minute film in the basement; ask for the English version. (Fee 15F. Verdun TI tel.
29-86-14-18, closes 12:00-14:00 except in summer.)
Before leaving, walk to the cemetery and listen for the
eerie buzz of silence and peace. Then visit the nearby
Tranchee des Baionnettes, where an entire division of
soldiers was buried alive in their trench.

Reims—Cathedral and Champagne
The cathedral of Reims is a glorious example of Gothic
architecture with the best west portal anywhere. (Medieval churches always face east; the end you enter is the
west portal.) The coronation place of 800 years of French
kings and queens, it houses many old treasures, not to

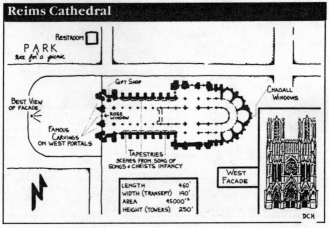

mention a lovely modern set of Marc Chagall stained-glass windows. (Open 8:00-21:00 daily.)

Reims is the capital of the Champagne region, and while the bubbly stuff's birthplace was Epernay, drivers save over an hour of road time by touring a champagne cave right in Reims. If you don't mind getting into Paris late (after rush hour), walk 10 minutes up rue de Barbatre from the cathedral to 9 place St. Nicaise (tel. 26-85-45-35) where the Taittinger Company will do a great job trying to convince you they're the best. After seeing their movie (in very comfortable theater seats), follow your guide down into some of the three miles of chilly, chalk caves, many dug by ancient Romans. Popping corks signal when the tour's done and the tasting's begun (15F, tours 9:30-11:30 and 14:00-16:00).

One block beyond Taittinger, on place des Droits de l'Homme, you'll find several other champagne firms. Most give free tours Monday through Saturday 9:00-11:00 and 14:00-17:00. I recommend Piper Heidsieck with its tacky train ride tour (51 boulevard Henri-Vasnier, tel. 26-85-01-94, free, but call first) and Veuve Clicquot-Pousardin (1 place des Droits de l'Homme, tel. 26-85-24-08).

Epernay—This town is the actual birthplace of champagne. It's the place where, in the 1600s, Dom Perignon shouted excitedly through the abbey, "Brothers, come quickly! I am drinking stars!" The best and bubbliest champagne tours are given right downtown by Moet et Chandon (20 avenue de Champagne, tel. 26-54-71-11, open daily with a break for lunch, free 45-minute English tours plus tasting; 9:30-11:30, 14:00-15:45). Why not celebrate with a bottle? Your tour is over, and you've just enjoyed France's best 22 days.

COMMUNICATING IN FRANCE

Those most interested in your money, the people you'll meet in more touristy areas, will probably speak some English, and you could manage much of this trip with the blunt weapon of English only. But those with an interest in speaking some French words will enjoy tremendous advantages—like better service, a friendlier reception, and getting what you ordered for dinner.

Learn the polite words—*pardon, bonjour, merçi*, and *s'il vous plaît*. With that as a base, carry a small English-French dictionary (the sturdy Collins-Gem is my favorite) or phrase book and a menu translator and make a point to learn and use five new words each day. Here are a few tips for the lazy linguist. Keep it simple, write things down on a pocket notepad, and let others communicate for you. If you're working with English, the first words out of your mouth should always be, "Bonjour Madame/Monsieur, parlez-vous anglais?" Then choose simple "Dick and Jane" words and pronounce every letter carefully; the person you're talking to most likely reads English better than he hears it.

Pronunciation tips:
■ Many letters are silent. Don't pronounce final consonants unless the next word begins with a vowel.
■ If a word ends with -*er*, -*et*, or -*ay*, it rhymes with "souflay."
■ Many English words (especially Latin root words ending in *ion*) can be Frenchified. So, nation = "nah-sheon."
■ Many English words ending in -*ive* are the same in French except they end in -*if*, like *adjectif* and *passif*.
■ Many modern words are universal—photocopy, TV, feedback, hamburger, and pique-nique.
■ Many foreign words are international—amigo, ciao, kaput.
■ Accents: the French language has more than its share of funny-looking marks over and under letters. They indicate the sound of the letter.

An acute accent over the letter *e*, as in été, means it is pronounced "ay" as in "*fate*." (The letter *e* at the end of a word is silent unless it has an acute accent.)

A grave accent over the letter *e*, as in père, means it is pronounced "eh" as in "met." The grave accent can also apprear over the letter *a* or *u*, where it distinguishes between words but does not change the sound of the vowel.

A circumflex accent over the letter *e*, as in crêpe, is pronounced "eh"—almost the same as è but held longer. It can also appear over other vowels. Hôtel is pronounced "hotel"; château "chateau."

A cedilla under the letter *c*, as in garçon, means it is pronounced like an *s*; otherwise, *c* sounds like *k* when it comes before the letter *a*, *o*, *u*, *n*, or *r*.

hello bonjour *bobn-ZHOOR*
good-bye au revoir *ob reb-VWAH*
see you later à bientôt *ab byunh-TOH*
good night bonne nuit *bobn NWEE*
please s'il vous plaît *seel voo PLAY*
thank you merçi *mebr-SEE*
yes/no oui/non *wee/nob*
one/two/three un/deux/trois *un/doo/twab*
cheap/expensive bon marché/cher *bobn mar-shay/shebr*
good/bad bon/mauvais *bobn/mo-VAY*
beautiful/ugly joli/laid *zbo-LEE/lay*
big/small grand/petit *grabn/peb-TEE*
fast/slow rapide/lent *rab-PEED/lab*
very très *tray*
Where is? Où est? *Oo ay*
How much? Combien? *kobm-bee-ab*
I don't understand Je ne comprends pas *zbub neb KOHM-prabn PAH*
What do you call this? Qu'est-ce que c'est? *KESS koo SAY?*
I'm lost. Je me suis perdu. *zbub meb suee pebr-DOO*
complete price (everything included) tout est compris *toot ay cobm-PREE*
I'm tired Je suis fatigué *zbub swee fab-tee-GAY*
I'm hungry. J'ai faim *zbay fab*
Cheers! Santé! *sabn-TAY*
food nourriture *new-ree-TOOR*
grocery store épicerie *eb-PEES-REE*
picnic pique-nique *peek-neek*
delicious délicieux *de-lee-syob*
market marché *mar-SHAY*
drunk soûl *SOO*
money argent *ar-ZHA*
station gare *gar*
private accommodations chambre *shambre*
I je *zbub*
you vous *voo*
love amour *ab-MOOR*
train train *tran*
The bill, please. L'addition, s'il vous plaît. *lab-dee-see-OHN, see voo play*
friend ami *ab-MEE*
water/tap water eau/eau douce *ob/OH doos*
castle château *sbat-TOH*
How are you? Ça va? *sab VAH*

I'm fine.   Ça va   *sah VAH*
Tourist Information   Syndicat d'Initiative   *san-dee-KAH-dee nee-see-ah-TEEV*

Hotel Talk
a room   une chambre
single/double/triple   single/double/triple
shower/bath   douche/bain
with/without   avec/sans
bathroom   salle de bain (not used if all you need is the toilet)
toilet   toilette/W.C. (pronounced "doo-bla vay-say")
bed   lit
no vacancy   complet
sleep   dormir
cheapest   le moins cher   *le mwah shehr*
with shower   avec douche   *a-veck doosh*
without   sans   *sahn*
double bed   grand lit   *grahn lee*
two small beds   deux petits lits   *doo peh-tee lee*
yes or no?   oui ou non?   *wee oh no?*
June   juin   *zhwann*
July   juillet   *zhwee-AY*
   (Most other months similar to English)
good   bon   *bohn*
okay?   d'accord?   *dack-KORR?*

Reserving a room by phone
Refer to hotel words above

Hello madam/sir. Do you speak English?
Bonjour, Madame/Monsieur. Parlez-vous anglais?
(Bone-ZHUR maw-DAM/mis-SYOOR, PAR-lay voo ong-GLAY?)

I would like a room for ___ persons (this evening/tomorrow/for the 5th of August) for ___ nights.
Je voudrais une chambre pour ___ personnes (ce soir/demain/pour la cinq août) pour ___ nuits.
(Zhuh voo-DRAY oon SHAWM-br uh poor ___ pair-SOHN [swah/duh-MANN/poor la sank oot] poor ___ nwee.)

With a bathroom/without a bathroom
Avec salle de bain/sans salle de bain
(Ah-veck sahl-duh-BANN/sahn sahl-duh-BANN.)

No problem?
Pas de problèmes?   (Pod prob-LEM?)

My name is Mr./Mrs./Miss ___ .
Je m'appelle Monsieur/Madame/Mademoiselle ___ .

(Zhuh mah-PELL Mis-SYOOR/maw-DAM/Mad-
mwah-ZELL ___ .)
(Note: If your real name is difficult for French people to
understand, pick an easy pseudonym, e.g., "Monsieur Jacques.")
I'll arrive about ___ o'clock.
Je vais arriver à ___ heures.
(Zuh vaiz arr-ree-vay-ah ___ err.)

Thank you. See you soon.
Merçi. A bientôt.
(Mehr-SEE. Ah byen-TOH.)

ALTERNATIVE ACCOMMODATIONS

Camping
Here are some good campgrounds along the route. All provide
free hot showers, clean bathroom facilities, and average 45F for
two per night. Campers should pack sleeping bags, tent, tarp,
sleeping pads, thongs for the showers, a camping *gaz* stove (no
showers, a camping *gaz* stove (no Coleman fuel here), a light
pot, plastic plates, and silverware. Consider buying cheap fold-
up camping chairs (40F), available at big French supermarchés.
   Paris: Avoid camping here. It's too hard to reach the city center. Still, if you must, try Camp du Bois du Boulogne, allée du
Bord de l'Eau in the Bois (woods) de Boulogne (tel. 45-24-30-00).
It's the only campground "in" Paris, but it is not strong on security and is generally crowded. Open all year and fully equipped.
Exit Périphérique at Porte Maillot.
   Rouen: Municipal Camping. Ten minutes by car or bus from
Rouen, in Deauville, on the N-15 toward Le Havre. Tel.
35-74-07-59. Nice but small area with immaculate bathrooms.
   Honfleur: Camping du Phare. A scruffy facility with a great
location—a few minutes stroll from the heart of Honfleur. It's
just outside the city as you head to Trouville. Open April
through October 15. A far nicer facility, but a five-minute drive
to town, is Camping Domaine Catinière, in Fiquefleur (tel.
32-57-63-51, open April through September).
   Bayeux: Municipal Camping. Very friendly, small sites but
terrific facility and a 10-minute walk to the city center. (Boulevard Eindhoven, tel. 31-92-08-43. Open March through
October 31.)
   D Day Beaches: You'll see small campgrounds everywhere.
The area between Arromanches and the Pointe du Hoc is best.
   Le Mont St. Michel: Camping du Mont St. Michel. (Pb.
8/50116 Le Mont St. Michel, tel. 33-60-09-33, check in at the
Motel Vert). It's 1.5 miles from Le Mont and 50 yards from great
views of it. Otherwise nothing to write home about. Open
year-round.

Amboise: Camping de L'Ile d'Or. On the island across the bridge from the city center, you can't miss it. Scenic location and easy walk into Amboise. Minigolf and pool (tel. 47-57-23-37).

Brantôme: Municipal Camping. Beautiful location and an easy walk to town. Tennis courts next door. (½ mile from town on the D-78 toward Thiviers. Tel. 53-05-75-24. Open June to September.)

Sarlat: Camping Les Perieres. A fifteen-minute walk downhill to Sarlat. This resort sports a pool, tennis courts, store, café, and lovely setting. Call ahead in the summer or forget it. (Rd. 47, tel. 53-59-05-84. Open April through September 30.)

Albi: Parc de Caussels. One mile east of town. Crowded but friendly, with a huge supermarket across the street (tel. 63-60-37-06. Open April to November).

Carcassonne: Camping de la Cité. Brand-new site and facility, 15-minute walk to la Cité. Inquire at TI for information or follow signs from the ville basse. (Tel. 68-25-11-77).

Avignon: Camping Bagatelle. Right across the Pont (bridge) Daladier from Avignon. Great city views, popular, but lots of sites, and a great café for making friends (tel. 90-86-30-39).

Arles: Camping City. The best and most convenient of several in the area. Fifteen-minute walk into the city center, a new pool, poolside café, and hairy umbrellas. (On the road to Crau, tel. 90-93-08-86. Open March to October 31.)

Cagnes-sur-Mer (Nice): Camping Panoramer. Meet the friendly owners and admire the best Riveria view around. It's a long walk to the Nice-bound bus stop, but they run often. (At chemin des Gros Buaux, tel. 93-31-16-15. Follow chemin du Val Fleuri from the N-7 in Cagnes-sur-Mer. Open Easter through September 20; call ahead in summer.)

Antibes: They're all over the place here. You'll see their signs. Easy access to Nice via a nearby bus. Arrive by noon in summer.

Chamonix: Camping les Rosières. Comfortable site, wonderful views and a beautiful 20-minute walk to town—follow the stream. Funky trailers for rent. One mile from Chamonix on the route du Praz (tel. 50-53-10-42; open all year).

Annecy: Campgrounds line each side of the lake—take your pick.

Beaune: Camping les Cent Vignes. This is my favorite campground of the trip, a 15-minute walk to the city center, fully equipped (great restaurant), individual sites, and campers from all over Europe. (10 rue Dubois, tel. 80-22-03-91. Follow signs toward Dijon and watch for camping signs. Open March 15 to October 31.)

Dijon: Camping Municipal du Lac. Streamside location and a short waddle to the lake. Fine facilities. (One mile from Dijon, follow signs from the station in the direction of Paris. Tel. 80-43-54-72. Open April to November 15.)

Colmar: Camping intercommunal de l'ile. A few miles from the city center but a nice riverfront location and good facilities. (Plage d'e l'ile, tel. 89-41-15-94. Follow the N-415 toward Fribourg. Open February to November 30.)

TELEPHONE DIRECTORY

Useful Parisian Phone Numbers and Addresses:
English tourist information recording: 47-20-88-98
American Express: 11 rue Scribe, Métro: Opera. 42-66-09-99
American Church: 47-05-07-99
American Hospital: 47-47-53-00
American Pharmacy: 47-42-49-40
Emergency: Dial 17 for police, otherwise 42-60-33-22
Office of American Services (lost passports, etc.): 42-96-12-02
U.S. Embassy: 42-96-12-02
Paris and France Directory Assistance (they speak some
    English): 12
Sunday Banks: 115 and 154 avenue des Champs-Élysées

Airline Offices in Paris:
Orly Airport Information: 48-84-32-10 or 49-75-52-52
Roissy-Charles de Gaulle Airport Information: 48-62-22-80
Air France: 43-35-61-61
American: 42-89-05-22
British Air: 47-78-14-14
Continental: 42-25-31-81
Delta: 43-35-40-80
KLM: 42-66-57-19
Lufthansa: 42-65-37-35
Pan Am: 42-66-45-45
SAS: 47-42-06-14
TWA: 47-60-62-11

City	Tourist Info	Train Info	Postal (Zip) Code
Paris	47-23-61-72 (usually speak English)	several stations (often do not speak English)	750XX (last 2 digits are arrondissement)
Rouen	35-71-41-77	35-98-50-50	76000
Honfleur	31-89-15-53		14600
Bayeux	31-92-16-26	31-92-80-50	14400
Mont St. Michel	33-60-14-30	33-60-10-97	(bus) 50016

City	Tourist Info	Train Info	Postal (Zip) Code
Amboise	47-57-09-28	47-20-50-50	37400
Brantôme	53-05-80-52	53-08-43-13	
Sarlat	53-59-27-67	53-90-00-21	24200
Albi	63-54-22-30	63-54-50-50	81000
Carcassonne	68-25-07-04	68-47-50-50	11000
Arles	90-96-29-35	90-93-74-90	(bus) 13200
Avignon	90-82-65-11	90-82-50-50	84000
Nice	93-87-07-07	98-87-50-50	06000
Chamonix	50-53-00-24	50-53-00-44.	74400
Beaune	80-22-24-51	80-44-50-50	21200
Dijon	80-43-42-12	80-41-50-50	21000
Colmar	89-41-02-29	89-41-66-80	68000
Verdun	29-84-18-85	29-86-25-65	55100
Reims	26-88-37-89	26-88-50-50	51084

Country Codes (when calling to. . .)

France 33	Germany 49
U.S.A. and Canada 1	Austria 43
Britain 44	Switzerland 41
Belgium 32	Italy 39
Netherlands 31	Spain 34

WEATHER

1st line, avg. daily low; 2nd line, avg. daily high; 3rd line, days of no rain

FRANCE
Paris

32°	34°	36°	41°	47°	52°	55°	55°	50°	44°	38°	33°
42°	45°	52°	60°	67°	73°	76°	75°	69°	59°	49°	43°
16	15	16	16	18	19	19	19	19	17	15	14

Nice

40°	41°	45°	49°	56°	62°	66°	66°	62°	55°	48°	43°
56°	56°	59°	64°	69°	76°	81°	81°	77°	70°	62°	58°
23	20	23	23	23	25	29	26	24	22	23	23

Train Route Map and Schedules

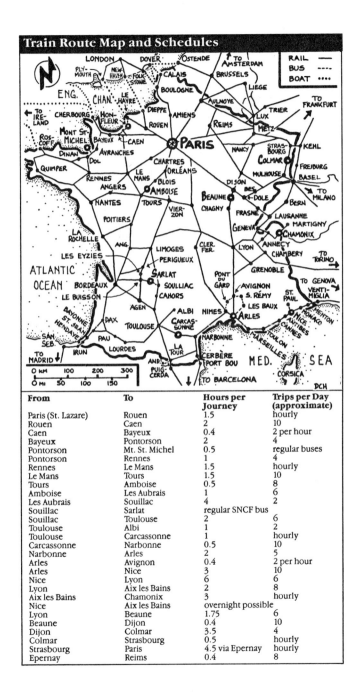

From	To	Hours per Journey	Trips per Day (approximate)
Paris (St. Lazare)	Rouen	1.5	hourly
Rouen	Caen	2	10
Caen	Bayeux	0.4	2 per hour
Bayeux	Pontorson	2	4
Pontorson	Mt. St. Michel	0.5	regular buses
Pontorson	Rennes	1	4
Rennes	Le Mans	1.5	hourly
Le Mans	Tours	1.5	10
Tours	Amboise	0.5	8
Amboise	Les Aubrais	1	6
Les Aubrais	Souillac	4	2
Souillac	Sarlat	regular SNCF bus	
Souillac	Toulouse	2	6
Toulouse	Albi	1	2
Toulouse	Carcassonne	1	hourly
Carcassonne	Narbonne	0.5	10
Narbonne	Arles	2	5
Arles	Avignon	0.4	2 per hour
Arles	Nice	3	10
Nice	Lyon	6	6
Lyon	Aix les Bains	2	8
Aix les Bains	Chamonix	3	hourly
Nice	Aix les Bains	overnight possible	
Lyon	Beaune	1.75	6
Beaune	Dijon	0.4	10
Dijon	Colmar	3.5	4
Colmar	Strasbourg	0.5	hourly
Strasbourg	Paris	4.5 via Epernay	hourly
Epernay	Reims	0.4	8

INDEX

Rick Steves' BACK DOOR CATALOG

*All items field tested, highly recommended, completely guaran-
teed, discounted below retail and ideal for independent, mobile
travelers. Prices include tax (if applicable), handling, and postage.*

The Back Door Suitcase / Rucksack $70.00

At 9"x22"x14" this specially designed, sturdy functional
bag is maximum carry-on-the-plane size (fits under the
seat) and your key to foot-loose and fancy-free travel.
Made of rugged water resistant Cordura nylon, it converts
easily from a smart-looking suitcase to a handy rucksack.
It has hide-away padded shoulder straps, top and side
handles and a detachable shoulder strap (for toting as a
suitcase). Lockable perimeter zippers allow easy access to
the roomy (2,700 cubic inches) central compartment. Two
large outside pockets are perfect for frequently used
items. Also included is one nylon stuff bag. Over 40,000 Back Door
travelers have used these bags around the world. Rick Steves helped design
and lives out of this bag for 3 months at a time. Comparable bags cost much
more. Available in navy blue, black, or grey.

Moneybelt $8.00

This required, ultra-light, sturdy, under-the-pants, nylon
pouch just big enough to carry the essentials (passport, air-
line ticket, travelers checks, and so on) comfortably. I'll
never travel without one and I hope you won't either. Beige,
nylon zipper, one size fits nearly all, with "manual."

Catalog   FREE

For a complete listing of all the books, travel videos,
products and services Rick Steves and Europe Through the
Back Door offer you, ask us for our 64-page catalog.

Eurailpasses . . .

...cost the same everywhere. We carefully examine each
order and include for no extra charge a 90-minute Rick
Steves VHS video Train User's Guide, helpful itinerary
advice, Eurail train schedule booklet and map, plus a free
22 Days book of your choice! Send us a check for the cost
of the pass(es) you want along with your legal name (as it
appears on your passport), a proposed itinerary (including
dates and places of entry and exit if known), choice of 22 Days book
(Europe, Brit, Spain/Port, Scand, France, or Germ/Switz/Aust) and a list of
questions. Within 2 weeks of receiving your order we'll send you your
pass(es) and any other information pertinent to your trip. Due to this unique service Rick Steves sells more passes than anyone on the West Coast
and you'll have an efficient and expertly-organized Eurail trip.

Back Door Tours

We encourage independent travel, but for those who want
a tour in the Back Door style, we do offer a 22-day "Best of
Europe" tour. For complete details, send for our free 64
page tour booklet/catalog.

*All orders will be processed within 2 weeks and include tax (where applicable),
shipping and a one year's subscription to our Back Door Travel newsletter.
Prices good through 1993. Rush orders add $5. Sorry, no credit cards. Send
checks to:*

**Europe Through The Back Door ● 120 Fourth Ave. N.
Box C-2009 ● Edmonds, WA 98020 ● (206) 771-8303**

Other Books from John Muir Publications

Adventure Vacations: From Trekking in New Guinea to Swimming in Siberia, Bangs 256 pp. $17.95

Asia Through the Back Door, 3rd ed., Steves and Gottberg 326 pp. $15.95

Belize: A Natural Destination, Mahler, Wotkyns, Schafer 304 pp. $16.95

Buddhist America: Centers, Retreats, Practices, Morreale 400 pp. $12.95

Bus Touring: Charter Vacations, U.S.A., Warren with Bloch 168 pp. $9.95

California Public Gardens: A Visitor's Guide, Sigg 304 pp. $16.95

Catholic America: Self-Renewal Centers and Retreats, Christian-Meyer 325 pp. $13.95

Costa Rica: A Natural Destination, Sheck 280 pp. $15.95 (2nd ed. available 3/92 $16.95)

Elderhostels: The Students' Choice, 2nd ed., Hyman 312 pp. $15.95

Environmental Vacations: Volunteer Projects to Save the Planet, Ocko 240 pp. $15.95 (2nd ed. available 2/92 $16.95)

Europe 101: History & Art for the Traveler, 4th ed., Steves and Openshaw 372 pp. $15.95

Europe Through the Back Door, 9th ed., Steves 432 pp. $16.95 (10th ed. available 1/92 $16.95)

Floating Vacations: River, Lake, and Ocean Adventures, White 256 pp. $17.95

Great Cities of Eastern Europe, Rapoport 240 pp. $16.95

Gypsying After 40: A Guide to Adventure and Self-Discovery, Harris 264 pp. $14.95

The Heart of Jerusalem, Nellhaus 336 pp. $12.95

Indian America: A Traveler's Companion, 2nd ed., Eagle/Walking Turtle 448 pp. $17.95

Mona Winks: Self-Guided Tours of Europe's Top Museums, Steves and Openshaw 456 pp. $14.95

Opera! The Guide to Western Europe's Great Houses, Zietz 296 pp. $18.95

Paintbrushes and Pistols: How the Taos Artists Sold the West, Taggett and Schwarz 280 pp. $17.95

The People's Guide to Mexico, 8th ed., Franz 608 pp. $17.95

The People's Guide to RV Camping in Mexico, Franz with Rogers 320 pp. $13.95

Ranch Vacations: The Complete Guide to Guest and Resort, Fly-Fishing, and Cross-Country Skiing Ranches, 2nd ed., Kilgore 396 pp. $18.95

The Shopper's Guide to Art and Crafts in the Hawaiian Islands, Schuchter 272 pp. $13.95

The Shopper's Guide to Mexico, Rogers and Rosa 224 pp. $9.95

Ski Tech's Guide to Equipment, Skiwear, and Accessories, ed. Tanler 144 pp. $11.95

Ski Tech's Guide to Maintenance and Repair, ed. Tanler 160 pp. $11.95

A Traveler's Guide to Asian Culture, Chambers 224 pp. $13.95

Traveler's Guide to Healing Centers and Retreats in North America, Rudee and Blease 240 pp. $11.95

Understanding Europeans, Miller 272 pp. $14.95

Undiscovered Islands of the Caribbean, 2nd ed., Willes 232 pp. $14.95

Undiscovered Islands of the Mediterranean, Moyer and Willes 232 pp. $14.95

Undiscovered Islands of the U.S. and Canadian West Coast, Moyer and Willes 208 pp. $12.95

A Viewer's Guide to Art: A Glossary of Gods, People, and Creatures, Shaw and Warren 144 pp. $10.95

2 to 22 Days Series
Each title offers 22 flexible daily itineraries that can be used to get the most out of vacations of any length. Included are not only "must see" attractions but also little-known villages and hidden "jewels" as well as valuable general information.

22 Days Around the World, 1992 ed., Rapoport and Willes 256 pp. $12.95

2 to 22 Days Around the Great Lakes, 1992 ed., Schuchter 192 pp. $9.95

22 Days in Alaska, Lanier 128 pp. $7.95

2 to 22 Days in the American Southwest, 1992 ed., Harris 176 pp. $9.95
2 to 22 Days in Asia, 1992 ed., Rapoport and Willes 176 pp. $9.95
2 to 22 Days in Australia, 1992 ed., Gottberg 192 pp. $9.95
22 Days in California, 2nd ed., Rapoport 176 pp. $9.95
22 Days in China, Duke and Victor 144 pp. $7.95
2 to 22 Days in Europe, 1992 ed., Steves 276 pp. $12.95
2 to 22 Days in Florida, 1992 ed., Harris 192 pp. $9.95
2 to 22 Days in France, 1992 ed., Steves 192 pp. $9.95
2 to 22 Days in Germany, Austria, & Switzerland, 1992 ed., Steves
224 pp. $9.95
2 to 22 Days in Great Britain, 1992 ed., Steves 192 pp. $9.95
2 to 22 Days in Hawaii, 1992 ed., Schuchter 176 pp. $9.95
22 Days in India, Mathur 136 pp. $7.95
22 Days in Japan, Old 136 pp. $7.95
22 Days in Mexico, 2nd ed., Rogers and Rosa 128 pp. $7.95
2 to 22 Days in New England, 1992 ed., Wright 192 pp. $9.95
2 to 22 Days in New Zealand, 1991 ed., Schuchter 176 pp. $9.95
2 to 22 Days in Norway, Sweden, & Denmark, 1992 ed., Steves 192 pp. $9.95
2 to 22 Days in the Pacific Northwest, 1992 ed. Harris 192 pp. $9.95
2 to 22 Days in the Rockies, 1992 ed. Rapoport 192 pp. $9.95
2 to 22 Days in Spain & Portugal, 1992 ed., Steves 192 pp. $9.95
22 Days in Texas, Harris 176 pp. $9.95
22 Days in Thailand, Richardson 176 pp. $9.95
22 Days in the West Indies, Morreale and Morreale 136 pp. $7.95

Parenting Series

Being a Father: Family, Work, and Self, *Mothering* Magazine 176 pp. $12.95

Preconception: A Woman's Guide to Preparing for Pregnancy and Parenthood, Aikey-Keller 232 pp. $14.95

Schooling at Home: Parents, Kids, and Learning, *Mothering* Magazine 264 pp. $14.95

Teens: A Fresh Look, *Mothering* Magazine 240 pp. $14.95

"Kidding Around" Travel Guides for Young Readers
Written for kids eight years of age and older.

Kidding Around Atlanta, Pedersen 64 pp. $9.95
Kidding Around Boston, Byers 64 pp. $9.95
Kidding Around Chicago, Davis 64 pp. $9.95
Kidding Around the Hawaiian Islands, Lovett 64 pp. $9.95
Kidding Around London, Lovett 64 pp. $9.95
Kidding Around Los Angeles, Cash 64 pp. $9.95
Kidding Around the National Parks of the Southwest, Lovett 108 pp. $12.95
Kidding Around New York City, Lovett 64 pp. $9.95
Kidding Around Paris, Clay 64 pp. $9.95
Kidding Around Philadelphia, Clay 64 pp. $9.95
Kidding Around San Diego, Luhrs 64 pp. $9.95
Kidding Around San Francisco, Zibart 64 pp. $9.95
Kidding Around Santa Fe, York 64 pp. $9.95
Kidding Around Seattle, Steves 64 pp. $9.95
Kidding Around Spain, Biggs 108 pp. $12.95
Kidding Around Washington, D.C., Pedersen 64 pp. $9.95

Environmental Books for Young Readers
Written for kids eight years of age and older.

The Indian Way: Learning to Communicate with Mother Earth, McLain
114 pp. $9.95

The Kids' Environment Book: What's Awry and Why, Pedersen 192 pp. $13.95

Rads, Ergs, and Cheeseburgers: The Kids' Guide to Energy and the Environment, Yanda 108 pp. $12.95

"Extremely Weird" Series for Young Readers
Written for kids eight years of age and older.
Extremely Weird Bats, Lovett 48 pp. $9.95
Extremely Weird Frogs, Lovett 48 pp. $9.95
Extremely Weird Primates, Lovett 48 pp. $9.95
Extremely Weird Reptiles, Lovett 48 pp. $9.95
Extremely Weird Spiders, Lovett 48 pp. $9.95

Quill Hedgehog Adventures Series
Written for kids eight years of age and older. Our new series of green fiction for
kids follows the adventures of Quill Hedgehog and his Animalfolk friends.
Quill's Adventures in the Great Beyond, Waddington-Feather
96 pp. $5.95
Quill's Adventures in Wasteland, Waddington-Feather 132 pp. $5.95
Quill's Adventures in Grozzieland, Waddington-Feather 132 pp. $5.95

Other Young Readers Titles
Kids Explore America's Hispanic Heritage, edited by Cozzens 112 pp. $7.95
(avail. 2/92)

Automotive Repair Manuals
How to Keep Your VW Alive, 14th ed., 440 pp. $21.95
How to Keep Your Subaru Alive 480 pp. $21.95
How to Keep Your Toyota Pickup Alive 392 pp. $21.95
How to Keep Your Datsun/Nissan Alive 544 pp. $21.95

Other Automotive Books
**The Greaseless Guide to Car Care Confidence: Take the Terror Out of Talking
to Your Mechanic,** Jackson 224 pp. $14.95
Off-Road Emergency Repair & Survival, Ristow 160 pp. $9.95

Ordering Information
If you cannot find our books in your local bookstore, you can order directly from us.
Please check the "Available" date above. If you send us money for a book not yet
available, we will hold your money until we can ship you the book. Your books will
be sent to you via UPS (for U.S. destinations). UPS will not deliver to a P.O. Box;
please give us a street address. Include $3.25 for the first item ordered and $.50 for
each additional item to cover shipping and handling costs. For airmail within the
U.S., enclose $4.00. All foreign orders will be shipped surface rate; please enclose
$3.00 for the first item and $1.00 for each additional item. Please inquire about foreign airmail rates.

Method of Payment
Your order may be paid by check, money order, or credit card. We cannot be
responsible for cash sent through the mail. All payments must be made in U.S. dollars drawn on a U.S. bank. Canadian postal money orders in U.S. dollars are
acceptable. For VISA, MasterCard, or American Express orders, include your card
number, expiration date, and your signature, or call (800) 888-7504. Books ordered
on American Express cards can be shipped only to the billing address of the card-
holder. Sorry, no C.O.D.'s. Residents of sunny New Mexico, add 5.875% tax to the
total.

Address all orders and inquiries to:
    John Muir Publications
    P.O. Box 613
    Santa Fe, NM 87504
    (505) 982-4078
    (800) 888-7504